THE OVERCOMER'S WAY TO GLORY

A Handbook of Victorious Holiness

by
Paul and Nuala O'Higgins

Published by
HUNTER BOOKS
City of Light
201 McClellan Road
Kingwood, Texas 77339,U.S.A.

ISBN 0-917726-72-3

Paul and Nuala O'Higgins may be reached by writing to:
RECONCILIATION OUTREACH, INC.
P.O. Box 2758
Stuart, Florida 33495

FOREWARD

I am happy to encourage you to study carefully what my precious friends, Paul and Nuala O'Higgins have written in "The Overcomers' Way To Glory". They present "the way, the truth, and life abundant" as it is in Christ in a clear, fresh and exciting way.

"The first man is of the earth, earthy; the second is the Lord from heaven. As is the earthy, such are they also that are earthy; and as is the heavenly, such are they also that are heavenly. As we have borne the image of the earthy, we shall also bear the image of the heavenly." (1 Corinthians 15:47-49)

"For God, who commanded the light to shine, hath shined in our hearts to give the light of the knowledge of the glory of God in the face of Jesus Christ. But we have this treasure in EARTHEN VESSELS, that the excellency of the power may be of God and not of us." (2 Corinthians 4:6-7)

"For as in Adam all die, even so in Christ shall all be made alive." (1 Corinthians 15:22)

The key phrase in the above scriptures is "EARTHEN VESSELS", that we may grasp the great truth of the prayer that Jesus taught us: *"Our Father, which art in heaven, hallowed be thy name. Thy kingdom come. Thy will be done IN EARTH, as it is in heaven."* His will cannot be done IN earth unless it is revealed in *earthen vessels*, that the excellency of the power may be of God. The kingdom of heaven is to be manifested on earth in and through earthen vessels, and that is the commission of Jesus' disciples.

When He met His ten disciples after His resurrection (John 20), He breathed the Holy Spirit into them, and said: Receive the Spirit and FORGIVE. This was the birth of a new body on earth: THE CHURCH. The first ministry was to forgive everybody. He had paid the price, and now the members of His Body on earth have the commission to offer UNCONDITIONAL FORGIVENESS.

Paul and Nuala in this book tell how Christ in us will manifest His GLORY and His KINGDOM in and through us, that we may become the answer to the prayer of Jesus in John 17:21: *"That they ALL may be one, as thou Father art one in Me, and I in Thee, that they also may be one in us, that the world may believe that thou hast sent me."* I heartily recommend this excellent 'handbook of victorious holiness' to the body of Christ and to all who would seek a fuller entry into and manifestation of the Kingdom of God on earth.

David J. du Plessis, D.D.

I yearn to see Paul & Nuala O'Higgins reproduce themselves throughout the Body of Christ. I pray that the clear revelation and teaching contained in their book, "The Overcomer's Way to Glory", will help achieve this end. It is exactly the teaching that is needed at this time."

Harald Bredesen

FOREWARD

The words in this book have been penned by individuals who have experienced the divine results of many varied tests and trials. Both Paul and Nuala have had years of training, study and practical ministry in the Roman Catholic Church, Paul as a priest and Nuala as a nun.

Several years after they had been born-again and baptised in the Holy Spirit, Paul and Nuala married and have become a tremendous team in teaching and ministering to God's people of all walks of faith. Today, this team is inspiring God's people around the world.

We have welcomed their warm spirits and anointed ability to teach regularly in our Institute of Ministry Training Schools at our Christian Retreat Center. Their own experiences and dedicated lives qualify them to write on the biblical principles of victorious Christian living.

This book will warm your heart, stirring you to holy living thus enabling you to enjoy God's special blessings. Allow it to be a study guide leading you into new heights with Jesus Christ. I feel it will be a great asset to the Body of Christ. As Christians we are all being changed from glory to glory. (II Corinthians 3:18)

Gerald Derstine, D.D.
President
Gospel Crusade, Inc.

TABLE OF CONTENTS

INTRODUCTION

"These men are turning the world upside down." This was the report that was passed around concerning the first Christians. In fact, God was turning the world upside down through them. Today once again, and more than ever, God is using ordinary people to turn the world upside down.

For a brief moment the world saw the Glory of God through and in the person of Jesus. Now through the Holy Spirit, that Glory is becoming manifest in every corner of the earth in the lives of millions.

The call begins with an invitation to receive the mercy of God through the cross of Jesus. Our life with Him begins with a discovery of Jesus as the Door. It proceeds with a life of obedience and union with Him as the Way and it is perfected when His Glory will swallow up all that is inglorious in us with His powerful presence. Finally, that presence of Christ that is now in us who believe in Him will break forth into full manifestation.

This process is taking place in our individual lives as believers, but it is also taking place in a global way throughout the earth. The life of Christ has been implanted in the hearts of millions of believers since the day of Jesus' resurrection. The kingdom of God is here already. It is here now in a hidden way, like leaven in a batch of bread, or salt in the stew. The hour is coming when all that veils the Glory of God from being seen on the earth will fall asunder and Christ shall be 'all in all'. We are the people of the Way on our way towards experiencing Glory in our lives and on the earth.

"The Glory which thou hast given me, I have given to them, that they may be one even as we are one, I in them and thou in me, that they may become perfectly one, so

that the world may know that thou hast sent me and hast loved them even as thou hast loved me" (John 17:22-23).

In our day this prayer is being answered. Millions of ordinary people today are presenting themselves to God that the life of Christ may come within them and that His Glory may be seen on the earth through them.

In this book, we are seeking to set forth some of the principles by which this great prayer of Jesus can be fulfilled in your life. The days of mere church membership are over. The days when believers would come to Jesus for forgiveness and nothing more are over. In these days we are becoming people of the Way once more. The church is 'rising' like Jesus from the tomb and throwing off the binding grave cloths of traditions and fear to move into the earth manifesting the radiant love and character of Jesus. The Glory that the world saw through Him will be seen again when His face is seen in our lives.

As Jesus brought the power and presence and rule of heaven to bear into the darkness and suffering of earth, so today God's people are being mobilized by the Holy Spirit to make His Light shine, and His Glory seen in every part of the world.

Heaven is invading earth with its warmth and healing; first in Jesus, then through those that are born of Him and walk His way on earth. As those who have come to Him as the Door surrender further to bear His life and walk His life as the Way, then the destination of Glory will be arrived at in our lives and in the earth. The Glory that is already given to us and already within us who believe is about to break forth in an unprecedented way on our earth. Heaven is coming to earth; first in Jesus, and now through Him in us!

PART I
THE DOOR - ENTERING IN

CHAPTER 1

RIGHT STANDING WITH GOD

As human beings, we know that there is something wrong with us. Each day we are bombarded with information that reminds us of this fact. We are conscious of an uneasy guilty feeling within us. We think that perhaps this feeling would go away if we had a better job, a smarter home, a nicer car, or if we were not so fat, short, tall, skinny, underprivileged, overprivileged or anything else that we are not now.

Sometimes we think that this uneasy feeling would go away if we could kick over the traces of rigid convention or the ethical codes of our society which we may regard as repressive.

On the other hand, there are those who seek release from their internal disease by conforming themselves blandly to the culture they find themselves in. Such people try to find acceptance by doing all the 'right' things, having all the 'right' things and going all the 'right' places.

That deep-seated feeling in all of us that something is the matter with us cannot be erased by any or all of these methods. The awareness just will not go away. All the money in the world, all the success in the world, all the social acceptance through conformity, fame or achievement, all the attempted escapes from conventional codes of morality and behavior cannot remove this sense that is deep-seated within everyone who comes into the world.

Preachers may tell us that what is wrong with us is that we are sinners. Very often that just makes us feel worse and even more hopeless and uneasy about our situation. We are not really interested in theological explanations. Oh yes, we do believe that God exists, but He is so impossible to please and so remote from our situation, we think it best to leave Him alone — if He will leave us alone.

However, God has decided not to leave us alone. He loves us and wants to be involved in our lives. Love would not be love if it did not reach out to help when it could. Love would not be love if it kept its distance when its closeness was needed. For this reason God has decided to involve Himself in our lives and in our history without violating the freedom He has given us to reject or to cooperate with Him and with His ways.

God began to reveal Himself in human history to the descendants of Adam, then more fully to Abraham and his son, Isaac and Isaac's son, Jacob. The descendants of these men became a special group of tribes with a special call to be the receptors of the Word of God.

Through Moses God revealed His way more fully to His people. He showed them that the origin of their problems was separation from Him and the consequence of this separation was death. He revealed to these people a strict code of ethics and conduct that would be pleasing to Him. However, again and again the people showed their inability to live by such high moral and spiritual standards. God knew that it would not be enough for Him to reveal to man His high and holy standards. He would also have to arrange provision for man when he would fail to meet these standards. God would have to give Himself fully in love without reservation to His creation, man, if he were to succeed in getting man to respond to Him in unreserved love. He would have to reveal something more than a moral standard. He would have to reveal His own Self.

"In many and various ways God spoke of old to our fathers by the prophets; but in these last days he has spoken to us by a Son, whom He appointed the heir of all things, through whom also He created the world. He reflects the glory of God and bears the very stamp of His nature, upholding the universe by His word of power" (Hebrews 1:1-3).

"And the Word became made flesh, and dwelt among us, full of grace and truth; ...And from His fulness have we all received grace upon grace. For the law was given through Moses; grace and truth came through Jesus Christ. No one has ever seen God; the only Son, who is in the bosom of the Father, He has made Him known" (John 1:14-16).

"For God so loved the world that He gave His only Son, that whoever believes in Him should not perish but have eternal life" (John 3:16).

Two thousand years ago, God sent His only Son into the world. God became man as a Jewish carpenter in Nazareth called Jesus. This man, who was God as man, died on the hill of Calvary outside Jerusalem. He became our substitute, dying in our place and taking on Himself our sin and the consequences of all of our inadequacies.

Through Moses and the prophets, God had revealed that the consequence of sin, spiritual and moral unwholeness, is death. The law and the prophets diagnosed our problem; however, it was through Jesus that God provided the healing prescription. God was sending Jesus into the world to take upon Himself the consequences of our sin so that we could be acquitted.

"The wages of sin is death" (Romans 6:23) but the free gift of God is eternal life in Christ Jesus. Through ourselves we earned death; through Jesus we are offered forgiveness and life.

The prophet Isaiah had prophesied this great event over seven hundred years earlier: *"All we like sheep have gone astray, we have turned everyone to his own way; and the Lord has laid on Him the iniquity of us all. ...Yet it was the will of the Lord to bruise him; he has put him to grief, when He makes himself an offering for sin ...by his knowledge shall the righteous one my servant, make many to be accounted righteous; and he shall bear their iniquities"* (Isaiah 53:6,10,11).

This amazing acquittal of the human race by the sacrifice which God Himself made through Jesus was accomplished for all of us two thousand years ago. All that is required of us now is that we accept this and live in the new kind of way that this acquittal has made possible.

Can you imagine a great balance scale? On the one side is all of our sins, inadequacies and shortcomings that have us weighed down with a sense of guilt, frustration and unworthiness before God. Even the most upright among us are imperfect and have fallen short of the standards of God. The best of us, no less than the worst of us, have enough on the debit side of the scale to balance it unfavorably against us.

As the apostle Paul puts it: *"All have sinned and all fall short of the glory of God"* (Romans 3:23). However, now we place the blood of Jesus on the other pan of the weighing scales. This perfect offering more than outweighs all the inadequacies and sins of both the worst of us and the best of us.

Spiritually, all our debts are paid in full by His great sacrifice for us. We are justified (acquitted) *"by his grace as a gift, through the redemption which is in Christ Jesus, whom God put forward as an expiation by His blood to be received by faith"* (Romans 3:24). The scales of justice have been eternally tipped in our favor by the work of Jesus on the cross!

Let us imagine a bottle of black ink spilt carelessly on a white table. The white table becomes black and stained. Now we take a sheet of pure white blotting paper and place it on the inky table. What happens? The table becomes white again and the blotting paper becomes black. The blotting paper has become black so that the table could become white again. The paper forfeits its own whiteness so that the table can regain its whiteness.

This is an exact parallel of what happens in the spiritual order when Jesus takes our sins upon Himself. He did this two thousand years ago, but it only becomes effective towards us when we apply its benefits to our lives through faith.

Paul puts it this way: *"For our sake he made him to be sin who knew no sin so that in Him we might become the righteousness of God"* (II Corinthians 5:21).

God loves us so much that He sent Jesus to take our appointment with judgement so that anyone who accepts the provisions of Jesus' death does not come into condemnation. We lived, as it were, on death row spiritually and Jesus came and took the execution for us so that we could go free without a record.

God accepts us into the realm of His love and grace not on the grounds of our goodness or badness, but on the grounds of the work of Jesus on the cross. Right standing with God is not a position one arrives at after years of religious activity, virtuous living, special meditation procedures or any such thing, but it is a gift already paid for that is freely available to every man, woman or child who will simply receive it.

There are only two sorts of people on the earth: those whom God loves and those who know it! There is no one that He does not love to the supreme extent. He is willing to give His Son as a ransom for everyone and has done so.

Though the sacrifice of Jesus was offered once for all men, it does not benefit any of us until we put our faith in it. Just like a check is of no benefit to us unless we cash it.

We cannot put our faith in the sacrifice of Jesus unless we are told about it. The realm of God's love is like a great banquet that has been freely opened up to all of us through the work of Jesus on the cross, but not everyone knows that they can freely enter and eat.

Once there was a very wealthy man who decided to use his money to help the hungry people in a part of Africa that had been devastated with severe famine. He set up a large soup kitchen in one of the villages and spread the word around the region that whoever needed food could come and eat.

Within a few weeks the hunger problem of the immediate area had virtually ceased. Only a few people in the area remained severely hungry. Most of these were people who, because of isolation, had not been told about the soup kitchen. There were also a few, who, though knowing that the food was freely available, were too proud to eat the food which the rich man had provided. These people were too proud to accept anything for which they could not pay.

The great tragedy today is that while God's love has been made freely available to all, not everybody knows about it. There are some who do know about it but refuse it preferring to attempt to make their way without God's assistance. There are some who do not know about the grace of God because they have never been told about it while others are hiding from God and acting as if He did not exist or was not interested in them. Still others refuse to be in debt to God and believe that they can please Him and get near to Him on the grounds of their good morality and conduct. These people are like starving people waiting to make themselves strong before they will approach the table for food.

This truth is also illustrated in the story of two young ladies who flew from a cold northern climate to the Caribbean for a winter vacation. They moved into their hotel room on the beach and their hearts rejoiced. They were going to spend the whole week on the beach soaking up the warm, friendly tanning rays of the sun and return to their northern city with a beautiful healthy tan.

However, when they looked out their window at the tanned bodies of the other sunbathers, they were too ashamed to go onto the beach in their bathing suits thinking they were too pale. As long as they remained in this fearful attitude, of course, they could never get a tan. After some time, their desire to enjoy the sun overcame their shame of coming boldly into the sunlight. When they first came out onto the beach, indeed, they were the palest ones there. However, within a few days they were as tan as anyone else there.

Many are afraid to come boldly into the light of God's wonderful love and grace because of a painful awareness of their inadequacy and unworthiness. If we wait until we are adequate or good enough, we will wait forever. If we do that, we would be like the pale sunbathers waiting until they are tanned before they appear in the sunlight.

Jesus has taken our sins and inadequacies on Himself so that we can come boldly into the realm of God's love and grace. *"Therefore, brethren, since we have confidence to enter the sanctuary by the blood of Jesus, by the new and living way which He opened for us through the curtain, that is through His flesh, and since we have a great priest over the house of God, let us draw near with a true heart in full assurance of faith..."* (Hebrews 10:19-21).

Jesus told a wonderful story about a young man who left home and spent all his money and energies on dissolute living. When he finally came to the pitiful end of his resources, he longed to return home but was quite fearful of doing so because of the disgraceful way that he had wasted his inheritance. When he finally did return home, his loving father treated him as if he had never done anything wrong and as if he had lived his whole life in complete perfection.

This is how God receives all who return to Him through the provision of Jesus. No matter how dissolute our past life has been, He chooses not to remember our sins and to accept us as if we had lived our whole lives in complete perfection. *" I will remember their sins no more,"* God promised through the prophet Jeremiah (Jeremiah 31:34).

How amazing is God's love and grace. He is not holding our sins against us. As we come to Him, He will cleanse us of all our mistakes and never remember them again. God has no second class members in His family. We can all draw very close to Him. When and if we sin, we should not run FROM Him but TO Him allowing Him to love us, forgive us and change us.

"Justified by faith we have peace with God through our Lord Jesus Christ....God's love has been poured into our hearts through the Holy Spirit which has been given us" (Romans 5:1,6). How wonderful when we let God forgive us and allow Him to flood our hearts with His love through the Holy Spirit.

God is not waiting for us to be good before He accepts us into His family and gives us the gift of right standing with Him. He offers us the gift of His love and forgiveness and perfect standing with Him no matter in what state of life we may be. Whether company president or skid row dropout, He makes the same offer freely to us all.

"While we were still weak, at the right time Christ died for the ungodly. Why, one will hardly die for a righteous man — though perhaps for a good man one will dare even to die. But God shows His love for us in that while we were yet sinners Christ died for us" (Romans 5:6-8).

There is no one on the face of the earth today, nor has there ever been, nor will there ever be anyone more loved by God than you! Our only responsibility is to 'soak it up' and respond to it. All barriers between us and this amazing love have been removed by Jesus on the cross. Those who come to God can come through Jesus into glorious realms of grace.

Any attempt to approach the love of God apart from the work of Jesus will fail. The veil of our sinfulness makes it impossible for us to stand in the pure light of God's love apart from the covering which God Himself provided for us when He appointed Jesus to bear our sins.

When a criminal escapes from the law and evades justice, deep inside himself he never feels free before the world and, in particular, before the representatives of the law, no matter how benign or loving they may be. Inside, his heart condemns him. However, if he goes to court and confesses his crime and is subsequently acquitted through mercy or serves his sentence, he no longer has that sense of guilt and fear upon his release.

Those who attempt to approach God's grace apart from the work of Jesus can never know the deep peace and cleansing of those of us who have confessed our sins and accepted the fact that Jesus has taken our sentence so that justice is satisfied. The sacrifice of Jesus and the shedding of His blood satisfies the holy standards of a righteous God. Eternal cosmic justice is satisfied perfectly by the sentence that Jesus bore.

It is important to make note at this point that God did not demand the death of Christ for us as if He were some vengeful executioner. To the contrary, He Himself was humbling Himself for us in Jesus, bearing on Himself the consequences of our self-destructive behavior so that we could be acquitted.

"God was in Christ reconciling the world to Himself, not counting their trespasses against them" (2 Corinthians 5:19). Like a courageous mother who steps in to protect her child from the bullets of an insane gunman, so God interposed Himself in Jesus between us and our sins.

By and large the full meaning of this amazing acquittal which gives us justification or right standing with God has not been fully appreciated and apprehended by most believers.

Righteousness means much more than the forgiveness of our sins. It is not just something that takes care of the negatives of our lives, but it is a positive new position before God. Not only does God acquit us of our sins, but He raises us up to share Jesus' very own relationship with Him. He adopts us into the royal family of heaven and puts in us the Spirit of Jesus. Not only does this King pardon His wrongdoer, but He makes him a part of His own royal family. We are not just forgiven humans, but humans who have been forgiven AND adopted into an altogether higher identity as sons of God. We are not just 'sinners saved by grace'. We once were sinners, but now through grace we have been given a new nature. Through Jesus, we who believe have the nature of God in us as well as the nature of man.

"He destined us in love to be his sons through Jesus Christ, according to the purpose of His will, to the praise of His glorious grace, which He freely bestowed on us in the Beloved. In Him we have redemption through his blood, the forgiveness of our trespasses, according to the riches of his grace which He lavished upon us" (Ephesians 1:5-8).

Jesus shares with us the very position that He alone enjoyed with the Father. He shares His Father with us making Him our Father, too. This puts us in a position of intimacy with God so that we can call Him 'Father'! *"And because you are sons, God has sent the Spirit of His son into our hearts, crying "Abba! Father! So through God you are no longer a slave but a son, and if a son, then an heir"* (Galatians 4:6-7).

This new awareness and reassuring confidence that becomes ours in our relationship with God enables us to go through the rest of our lives with the happy awareness that we are continually surrounded by His love, care and benign activity.

To be righteous, then, means much more than acquittal and forgiveness of our sins. It is the ability to stand in God's presence without any sense of inferiority, guilt or condemnation — — in awe, yes, but in trepidation, no.

"There is no fear in love, but perfect love casts out fear. For fear has to do with punishment, and he who fears is not perfected in love" (I John 4:18). Indeed, we can actually dare to say that the gift of righteousness — right standing with God — gives us the ability to stand in God's presence as if we were Jesus. This is why believers in Jesus can pray 'in the Name of Jesus' because He has lifted us up to share His own Sonship.

"His divine power has granted to us all things pertaining to life and godliness, through the knowledge of him who has called to his own glory and excellence, by which he has granted to us his precious and very great promises, that through these you may escape from the corruption that is in the world because of passion and become partakers of the divine nature" (II Peter 1:3-4).

This righteousness which has been made available to all must be appropriated by each one individually through faith. To do this we must put our faith in God's plan through Jesus and come close to Him through Jesus' atoning work. Just as an entrance ticket to the theatre is worthless if the bearer does not use it to enter the theatre and attend the concert, so too the work of Jesus on the cross is of no avail to us unless we boldly put our faith in it and enter into a life of fellowship and closeness to God our Father.

Faith, then, is more than the intellectual belief in the efficacy of Jesus' work but the act of 'using' what Jesus accomplished on the cross as the gateway to a life of undeserved blessings from God whereby we allow Him to love us and we love Him in return. The ticket holder puts his faith in the ticket, not when he accepts the ticket but when he uses it to enter the theatre.

Many today have a mere intellectual faith in the work of Jesus but are not really using it to enter into a life of fellowship with God. They are like ticket holders who have never entered the theatre.

Let us be sure to enter the kingdom of God through the work of Jesus. This is our highest destiny and is the greatest thing that can happen to anyone. The experience of it is better than the reports of it!

A PRAYER

Heavenly Father, thank you for sending Jesus to take my sin and my guilt on His own shoulders. Thank you that through Him I can come home to your love and grace. I acknowledge my need for Him to bear the burden of my sin and I now recognize that He has already done what was necessary for my atonement.

I thank You, Jesus, for being my Savior. Through You I approach Your Father as my Father. And I ask You, Father, to let me experience Your love and Your grace at work in my life every day. Transform me now as I lay down my sin at the feet of Jesus and as I allow His great sacrifice on the cross to be the paper to blot out my sin. Put the Spirit of Jesus within me and cause me to be pleasing to You in every way. Amen.

CHAPTER 2

THE CALL TO REPENTANCE

Most of us, when we hear the word 'repent' have an inherent tendency to want to hide or run away in the hope against hope that the challenge is not being directed to us. We associate the word with condemnation. Like naughty schoolboys seeking to hide from the accusing finger of the all-seeing schoolteacher, we fear the call to repentance.

Yet the ministry of Jesus was not to condemn the world, but to save the world; not to condemn sinners but to befriend and heal them. It is He that sounds the clearest call to repentance that the world has ever heard.

The Good News begins with a call to repentance: *"Repent, and believe the good news. The time is fulfilled and the kingdom of God is at hand"* (Mark 1:15). These are the first words of Jesus that are recorded in Mark's gospel. This call to repentance is not the cry of the 'finger pointer' but it is the cry of one who is offering a great new beginning to mankind in general and every individual in particular.

The call to repentance is a simple, direct call to change — to drop the old in favor of an altogether superior way of living. When our advertising men today herald the arrival of a new product that makes similar products obsolete, they are in fact calling us to repent from our old product, our old way of washing, or dressing, or eating, or whatever they are advertising, to a new and better way of doing that activity.

Likewise, the call to repentance is not just a negative call that criticizes and condemns our old way of living, but it is a call to accept a wonderful alternative to our old ineffective, destructive, self-orientated, self-dependent way of living. In fact, it is only when something better is presented to us that we can change from the old to the new. It is only when we actually see that the new is better that we can be willing to make the switch. To repent is to switch from an old way of living to a new way of living after the new way is discovered to be more desirable and better than the old way.

Once there was a young man who was the proud owner of a very dilapidated old car. He was very attached to this car even though it was far from being roadworthy. Indeed, his brothers referred to it as 'an accident looking for a place to happen'. His friends constantly urged him to get rid of the disgraceful wreck, and his parents had become quite concerned that the car could bring about his death some day. Time went by and still the young man refused to heed his friends' and parents' warnings. Their persistent warnings had not succeeded in getting him to change.

One day, however, the young man's parents came up

with a wonderful solution, though a costly one. They decided to buy their son a brand new car and to give it to him as a gift. As soon as their son saw the new car and was told that it was a gift from his loving parents, he was elated.

"This is wonderful!" he exclaimed as he jumped in behind the wheel. He never drove or even thought about his old car again.

"The kingdom of heaven is like treasure hidden in a field," said Jesus, *"which a man found and covered up; then in his joy he goes and sells all that he has and buys that field." "Again,"* He said, *"the kingdom of heaven is like a merchant in search of fine pearls, who, in finding one pearl of great value, went and sold all that he had and bought it"* (Matthew 13:44-45).

When the Holy Spirit shows us what the kingdom of God is really like, we too will want to sell out. This is real repentance.

We have taught repentance so much in negative terms, that we have missed the fact that it is essentially a call to accept, or to get ready to accept something that is infinitely more valuable and worthwhile than anything we may have to give up.

To repent means to change one's mind and heart. The mind and will can only be changed when they are presented with something that they perceive to be better than that to which they had been attached. Modern psychology has confirmed what was always suspected, that where there is a clash between our wills and our desires, our desires always 'win'. It is not until the desires are shown something more desirable than that which has previously drawn them that the will can choose to change.

The offer of the kingdom of God is the highest and

most desirable offer that could be made to us. When faced with the presentation of its claims, it is not difficult for us to leave our lower forms of living as separated self-dependant beings and to change to a life of union and friendship with God under His benign care, protection and provision.

This was the repentance that Jesus preached. His is not the voice of the nagging complainer, but the joyful voice of the herald of good news. His is a call to come away from the insufficiencies of our separated lives and to come into the all sufficiency of the love and care of God.

In the process of coming to Him, there is, of course, an admission of the insufficiency of the old life and of its inadequacy and its failure to deeply satisfy; but this confession comes simultaneously with the joyful acceptance of the new order. The returning prodigal, who represents all of us who have gone our own way, is more conscious of returning to the shelter and love of his father than he is of leaving his old frustrating way of living.

We often think of repentance as something that simply applies to 'bad' people. We think of it as something that takes place when 'bad' people finally decide to straighten up, or perhaps as something that takes place when one of us decides to give up some bad habit. The repentance that Jesus calls us to, however, goes far deeper than that. It goes far deeper than turning away from bad habits and ways.

He was constantly pointing out that those who lived 'good' lives and who were respectable law-abiding citizens were in just as great a need of repentance as were the more obvious sinners. Jesus said: *"Truly, I say to you, the tax collectors and the harlots go into the kingdom of God before you. For John came to you in the way of right-*

eousness, and you did not believe him, but the tax collectors and the harlots believed him" (Matthew 21:31-32).

Jesus is pointing out how difficult it is for people who are living what we would call 'good' lives to recognize that they are in need of repentance. Such people find it hard to recognize their need of repentance because they are, they believe, doing alright and making a good success of their lives apart from the direct mercy and aid of God.

The 'bad' people, on the other hand, keep getting themselves into trouble and so they can more readily recognize that they need God's mercy and help. They easily recognize that the life that is built on 'self' is unsatisfying and unsatisfactory. These people find it easier to abandon their independent self-propelled way of living and to thrust themselves on the mercy, love and care of God and receive from Him the ability to live in a new way.

"Those who are well have no need of a physician, but those who are sick" (Mark 2:17). Those who do not realize that they are sick will never make themselves available to the healing work of the physician.

Repentance, then, is not merely the changing from 'bad' behavior to 'good' behavior, but the change from a life that is lived by the power of SELF to a life that is lived by complete and total dependance on God. It is the change from a 'self' life (whether that self is 'good' or 'bad') to a 'Christ' life.

Real repentance, as Jesus preached it, goes beyond the awareness that there is something wrong with our behavior to an admission that we need God's forgiveness, and not only His forgiveness, but His presence and His very life to uphold us in every area of our lives. This is why the first description Jesus gives of the people who will receive the kingdom of God is that they are those who are 'poor in spirit'. This indicates those who are poignantly aware of their need of God. Those who cannot live without God and who do not wish to do so, are the kind of people who are candidates for the kingdom of God.

Real repentance is totally different from any self-righteous resolve to do better or to pull ourselves together. It can only be brought about by the Holy Spirit. It only comes about when we realize our radical inability to meet God's holy standards for us apart from His mercy and continuous direct enablement. Only the Holy Spirit can show us this. It comes about when we realize that it is not just our behavior that is or has been lacking but that the problem is even deeper than our behavior —— the problem is with US.

It is we ourselves who are the problem and not just our conduct. We can only have the kind of repentance Jesus calls for when we realize that apart from God's direct presence and activity in our lives, we fall short. Only then can we make the kind of repentance Jesus calls us to. This is the real switch of repentance, not merely from bad behavior to good behavior, but from lives empowered by self to lives empowered by God. It is this kind of repentance that 'good' people need as much as 'bad' people.

Jesus promised that He would send the Holy Spirit to convict the world of sin. We are often too blind, complacent or self-sufficient even to realize that it is we who are the ones who stand in the need of the mercy of God to forgive us, the grace of God to change us and the continuous presence of God to keep us.

In real repentance, then, we go far beyond the act of making good resolutions. When we see the inadequacy of our old lives which have been lived in the power of self, we can ask God's forgiveness, accept it and receive from Jesus His own life to come within us to empower us for a whole new life. We then live no longer by the power of ourselves, but by the power of His presence with us and in us.

"Have mercy on me, O God, according to thy stead-fast love; according to thy abundant mercy, blot out my transgressions. Wash me thoroughly from my iniquity, and cleanse me from my sin!"

"...Create in me a clean heart, O God, and put a new and right spirit within me. Cast me not away from thy presence, and take not thy holy Spirit from me" (Psalms 51:1-2,10-11).

In the kingdom of God there are no self-righteous people, but only those who have realized that they cannot make it apart from the direct presence of God with them continuously, and apart from the gift of His mercy and of the new life which He gives.

Jesus said that apart from His continuous presence with us, we could do nothing (John 15:5). The converse side of this is that apart from Him He does not expect us to do anything or to be able to do anything. When we discover that our lives do not amount to anything of lasting value apart from Him, we are ready to be joined to Him. As the finger cannot function apart from the hand, but becomes weak and lifeless, so man cannot function as his Creator intends him to, as long as he remains separated from Him.

Repentance goes beyond the mere modification of our behavior. It consists in coming away from our separation from God. *"I am the true vine,"* Jesus says, *"and my Father is the vinedresser. ...As the branch cannot bear fruit by itself unless it abides in the vine, neither can you unless you abide in me. I am the vine, you are the*

*branches. He who abides in me, and I in him, he it is that
bears much fruit, for apart from me you can do nothing. If
a man does not abide in me, he is cast forth as a branch
and withers; and the branches are gathered, thrown into
the fire and burned"* (John 15:1,4-6).

In calling us to repentance, then, God is not scolding
us, but calling us away from a life of fruitlessness, that is
withered spiritually. He is calling us away from the
loneliness of our pride and self-sufficiency to receive the
free forgiveness of our sins. He is calling us to allow His
love and His Spirit to make us over and equip us for a
wonderful new life under the captaincy of Jesus in union
with Himself.

A PRAYER

*Father, forgive me for trying to make it on my
own. I need you. I need your forgiveness. I need
your presence and power to sustain me every
moment of the day. I ask you to give me the new
life of the Holy Spirit that I may no longer live
from the 'engine' of my own self but from the
'engine' of Your Spirit. I ask you, Jesus, to take
the 'steering wheel' of my life that my life can be
lived under Your control, no longer for my own
purposes and ends but for Your goals and ends.
I let go living by the power of myself and I come
home to You, Father, to live the rest of my life
under the shelter of Your care, Your provision
and Your grace.*

CHAPTER 3

FAITH WITHOUT RELIGION

Dietrich Bonhoffer, a great twentieth century German theologian, coined the phrase 'religionless Christianity'. There is much truth in that phrase. Although sociologists and others count Christianity as a great religion, in fact, it is not a religion at all.

Religion is man's effort to improve himself through willpower or some other techniques in order to please God. Religion is man's effort to reach up to God to find favor with Him. Sometimes in this effort to reach God we can get ourselves into the most bizarre situations. People who pursue God along this line almost invariably end up in a kind of fanaticism and can find themselves doing the most ridiculous things to attain their goals of reaching or finding favor with God. This kind of religion is ultimately doomed to confusion and futility.

The scriptures record one such group of zealous

people who tried to reach God through their own efforts and energies. These people set out to build a tower that reached to Heaven. Their project was built on their own prowess and ingenuity. It was to be a monument to their own greatness and skill.

"*Then they said, 'Come, let us build ourselves a city, and a tower with its top in the heavens, and let us make a name for ourselves, lest we be scattered abroad upon the face of the whole earth.' And the Lord came down to see the city and the tower, which the sons of men had built. And the Lord said, 'Behold, they are one people, and they have all one language; and this is only the beginning of what they will do, and nothing that they propose to do will now be impossible for them. Come let us go down, and there confuse their language, that they may not understand one another's speech.' So the Lord scattered them abroad from there over the face of all the earth*" (Genesis 11:4-8).

The Babylonians in this event are a symbol of all self-made men. They are types of all who try to build their lives on their own selves. In God's kingdom there are no self-made men, only those who have allowed God to make something out of their lives. There is a life that we can make for ourselves, and there is a life which God will make for us; and the two are quite different.

The book of Genesis also recounts the call of Abraham. His life is in complete contrast to the Babylonian way. He is a type and model of all men of faith, of all whose life is a product of God's blessing rather than their own prowess. Abraham, in complete contrast to the men of Babylon, set out to have his life planned and built by God.

"*He looked for a 'city which has foundations whose builder and maker is God*'" (Hebrews 11:10). When God called him, God said to him: *"I will make you a great nation, and I will bless you, and make your name great, so that you will be a blessing"* (Genesis 12:2).

Many people are under the impression that if we direct our ambitions towards making ourselves very godly, we are thereby being involved in very godly activity. The self-made man is found pre-eminently in the business world but also in the world of religious pursuit. The Babylonians were, after all, trying to build a tower to reach to heaven. So much of what goes by the name of piety and genuine religion today is simply the tower of Babel all over again...that is, man by his own efforts and through his own skill and intelligence trying to measure up to God's heights.

The kingdom of God comes as such a contrast to all of this that, to many, it is a scandal and an affront. The kingdom that Jesus announced and brought was for the poor in spirit, the meek, the hungering after righteousness. Those who would receive His kingdom would be those who were all too painfully aware of their need of God's mercy and grace. They would be those who were deeply conscious of their own inability to please God apart from the direct intervention of God Himself.

The kingdom of God is not a plateau to which man can climb, but it consists of a radical breaking into a man's life of the living God who can make him something and somebody which he could never make himself into.

The kingdom of God is for those, like Abraham, who are aware of the inadequacy of anything that is built simply on the power of man. It is for those who know that even the most secular activity will come to confusion and frustration unless it has God as its foundation and builder. The kingdom of God is for those who are aware that man cannot please God without God stooping down to lift him up.

Today we live in an age of almost unprecedented confidence in our own systems and cleverness. There are signs, however, that such confidence is beginning to fade. Our science and technology and social management have not brought Utopia. We live in a time of increasing uneasiness, with social and moral problems equal to those of any previous generation. The way of self-reliance which thinks we could build our own paradise is beginning to come to a new point of confusion.

But is there an alternative to the strain of a life that is built on self? As the signs of the crumbling of Babylon appear, there are also signs of a tremendous rediscovery of the way of Abraham, the way of faith and of the kingdom of God that Jesus brought.

God, seeing the futility of Babylon, allows our prideful self-confidence to come to naught, be it in the sphere of politics, commerce, the social sciences, or religion that we exercise our self-reliance. God Himself is becoming active in the affairs of all who will permit Him to act as the shaper of their destiny. All who turn away from self-dependence can receive from Him a new blueprint of a new project which He has for our individual and collective lives.

What has He in mind for our lives? We have tried like the Babylonians to make a name for ourselves, but what is the name He could make for us? What are the plans and projects and destinies into which He could cause us to come?

Those who are becoming what God wants them to be, through following Jesus, are not mere products of their culture and heredity but products of His refashioning. Those who do not follow, not only miss the kingdom of God on earth but also the greatest adventure and romance on earth. Abraham discovered this when he left his Babylonian culture behind. The disciples discovered this on that great day in their lives when they came face to face with Jesus who called them to follow, forsake, and become.

Leaving Babylon

To the person who is still trying to build his own life by his own power, repentance means to try harder and harder. It means to pull oneself up by one's own bootstraps, to make something even more of yourself. It is no wonder that when we hear such calls to repentance, we almost instinctively recoil from them.

Often because 'good' people go to a church or synagogue, work hard every day, do not rob or commit adultery, pay their taxes and give some charitable donations, they are so good that they do not see that they are in need of the help of God. They don't realize that they need the presence of God, the life of God and the power of God for their lives to be what they should be. As good as these people's lives are, they are not yet what God wants them to be. There is so much more they can never experience unless they call out to God.

Jesus told a story about two men who went to pray in order to fulfill their religious duties. *"He also told this story to some who trusted in themselves that they were righteous and despised others: 'Two men went up into the temple to pray, one a Pharisee and the other a tax-collector. The Pharisee stood and prayed thus with himself, 'God, I thank thee that I am not like other men, extortioners, unjust, adulterers, or even like this tax-collector. I fast twice a week, I give tithes of all that I get.'*

But the tax-collector, standing far off would not even lift up his eyes to heaven, but beat his breast saying, 'God be merciful to me a sinner!'...I tell you," says Jesus, *"this man went down to his house justified rather than the other"* (Luke 18:9-14).

One of the many lessons this parable contains is that good self-righteous people are in as great a need of repentance as the more obvious sinner. Repentance is not a matter of changing from a bad life to a good life, but from a life lived by the power of self to a life that is lived by the power of Christ.

In Christian repentance we lay down our old separated life and pick up as a gift, the new life of Christ. That old self-life may have been good, very good, but it is still short of God's best. Many people have the idea that repentance is simply a matter of stopping 'bad' activity and trying to do 'good' things instead. This idea has done tremendous damage to our church life. Millions have been assured that they had indeed repented when they had, in fact, just become self-righteous.

Repentance is NOT a matter of ceasing to do bad things, but it is a matter of ceasing to live from the power of self and drawing from the ever available presence and power of God Himself.

There are countless thousands today who believe they are working for God and who don't do obviously bad things. They are convinced that they have repented when in fact they never have done so. These are the ones who believe they are working FOR God in what they do. They believe they are doing their part for God and performing their duties as good citizens and good Christians.

Such people have gone no further than the builders of the tower of Babel. The product of their labors will be no more valuable to God than the product of the work by the men who built that confusing tower. They have never really repented, probably through no fault of their own except that they trusted too much on themselves just like the Pharisee in Jesus' story.

As long as we are building on self, we have not repented. To repent is to look to the power, person and presence of God to act for us, with us, and through us, and to learn to put no confidence in anything which has not had its origin in Him.

Jesus said that everyone who heard and acted in accordance with His instructions would be like *"a wise man who built his house upon the rock; and the rain fell, and the floods came, and the winds blew and beat upon that house, but it did not fall, because it had been founded on the rock. And everyone who hears these words of mine and does not do them will be like a foolish man who built his house upon the sand; and the rain fell and the floods came, and the winds blew and beat against that house, and it fell; and great was the fall of it"* (Matthew 7:24-27).

In the book of Revelation, John saw Babylon had fallen. In his letters Paul warns his readers at Corinth that they must come out of Babylon and have no part in it. Babylon here is not meant to be taken as the literal city of Babylon for at the time of Paul and John, that city was already in ruins and nobody was living in it so certainly the Corinthians who lived at Corinth were not living there.

Babylon is not a place or a denomination or an organization of any sort in the context in which Paul and John speak, rather it is a symbol for all the work and lives that are not built on the power of God and the rock of Christ. What is built on self in your life and my life is doomed to destruction and confusion as was the tower of

Babel, but what is built on God's Word and His promises (as Abraham's life was) will endure forever. The winds of time and the rains of adversity will not destroy that which is built on God, His promise and the power and work of Jesus.

Much of what is called Christianity today is in fact nothing more than another tower of Babel decorated with Christian symbols, and the foundation is still self. However, in the midst of all of this, God is drawing to Himself a humble people who are, like Abraham, building their lives on Christ and God's promises and not on their selves. These are the ones who are experiencing the kingdom of God in reality today. They make up the true church. Babylon today is found, to some extent, in almost every denomination and Christian organization.

The kingdom of God can also be found in these same places. The difference is not so much in the activity but in the source of those activities. Is the source of these activities God, or do these activities have their origin in the will of man? All activity that has its origin in the will and ambition of man will go the way of the tower of Babel, even if that activity is religious or pious activity.

Today more than ever when technology has placed at our disposal such amazing resources, we need to be unusually discerning in our assessment of religious movements. Size of crowds, financial success, widespread reputation, none of these are adequate criteria for discerning whether any particular project has its origin in God or in man.

The people at Babel were highly successful in what they were doing, but their project had its origin in the pride of man and its power in the ingenuity of man. Now, God may use, and will use, the ingenuity of men; but when we act apart from Him, He considers our work to be nothing.

"Apart from me you can do nothing," says Jesus (John 15:5). That is, anything done apart from Him is considered by Him to be nothing, no matter how big or religious that project is. Even the use of the name of God and Bible terminology is no guarantee that the project has God as its source. To add God's name to our projects still will not make them His projects. To do this is to take His name in vain.

"Not everyone who says to me 'Lord, Lord,' shall enter the kingdom of heaven, but he who does the will of my Father who is in heaven. On that day many will say to me, 'Lord, Lord, did we not prophesy in Your name and cast out demons in your name, and do many mighty works in your name?' And then will I declare to them, 'I never knew you; depart from me, you evildoers" (Matthew 7:21-23).

Such works and projects, even when they are religious works and projects that have been done out of the initiative, ambition and pride of man, are what the scriptures call 'dead works'. In these last days when we are promised that lawlessness would abound, the earth is filled with the noise and clamor of these dead works. Some of these 'dead works' may look anything but dead. Such works bring with them a noisy and frantic activity, the same kind of noisy excitement and bustle that filled the city when the builders of Babel were at work.

Let us be careful that we do not get seduced by such empty and feverish activity which goes on in the Lord's name, and confuse it with the work of the Lord. Two men can be involved in the same church or in the same Christian evangelism program or the same inspirational publishing or broadcasting, one of whom is there by the leading of the Spirit, and the other by the leading of his carnal ambition. One is involved in a 'dead work' and the other in a living ministry.

Let us leave Babylon. Leave the activity that has its origin in our natural selves and be alive and attentive to do those things that proceed from God, building our lives on the foundation of His care and His promises.

'Follow Me and I Will Make You...'

When Jesus called His first disciples, He said to them what He says to you: *"Follow me and I will make you..."*(Mark 1:17). He was calling those first disciples to leave what they were in the world for the sake of what He could make of them. He was calling them away from the life they could make for themselves to the life He was choosing for them.

Those men like you and I, were the product of their culture and their education, of their family life styles and their religious backgrounds. A sociologist could have made many projections about the way their lives would turn out. When these men encountered Jesus, the living Word of God, they were challenged to leave what they could make of themselves and what others expected them to make of themselves, follow Him and allow Him to make something altogether different of their lives.

The adventure of discipleship is that we learn to surrender our lives to the one who loves us most, God in the person of His Son. By following and forsaking we are refashioned and remolded by Him to be the kinds of people that He has in mind for us to become. If this path is faithfully followed by anyone who comes after Jesus as a disciple and remains obedient to the Holy Spirit and the experiences he is led into, such a person will be reshaped to be just like Jesus.

The life of discipleship is a forsaking of all our Babylons, all our selfish ambitions, and all our goals that conflict with His goal. Follow Him and in the process become a different kind of person.

Jesus was not saying: "Make yourself something and then come and follow me." He was saying, "Follow me and I will make you into the kind of person I have destined you to become." He does not give us a blueprint for self-reconstruction, but just tells us to follow Him with the promise that if we do follow, He will make us over.

We tear up our limited blueprint for our own lives and follow Him without fully seeing the blueprint from which He is working. This call to discipleship is, of course, a call to all believers. Those who through fear or unwillingness prefer to stay with their own plans for their lives, miss not only the rewards of His kingdom but the great adventure of following Him and becoming more and more like Him through the refashioning work of the Holy Spirit.

The kingdom of God is not for the 'self made' men, but is found in the hearts and lives of all of those in every denomination (and outside of them) who are genuinely building their lives on the promises of God.

Most of the secular world, of course, consists of that which is built on the power of man rather than the power of God. For this reason we have sometimes been led to believe that involvement with secular activity could never be God's highest and best for any life. However, secular activity can be as blessed as Church activity if that work has its origin in the promises of God more than the prowess of man. *"Unless the Lord builds the house, those who build it labor in vain"* (Psalm 127:1).

It is not whether a work is secular or religious that makes it valuable or worthless to God, but whether or not He is the author and the power behind the work. It is not whether it is secular or religious that gives a work its worth but whether it is built by God or by man.

Coming away from dependance on self and learning to build our whole lives with its many facets and components on the grace, power, and person of God brings us into a living experience of the kingdom in *all* that we do.

To come away from Babylon is to cease from those activities which are built on the power of self for the glory of self (secular or religious). Like Jesus, we are called to leave all that we can do by the power of self, (even the good and religious things we could do by the power of self) and do only those things which God wants us to do and which He does with us and through us. *"Truly, truly, I say to you, the Son can do nothing of his own accord, but only what he sees the Father doing; for whatever he does, that the Son does likewise"* (John 5:19).

CHAPTER 4

THE GIFT OF NEW LIFE

We have seen how God made provision for the forgiveness of our sins, enabling us to approach Him and receive His love and grace. God, however, has an even greater purpose for us than this. He wants and has provided the means for us to grow to be more and more like Him.

God expects all of us who have been adopted into His royal family to allow our conduct and character to be changed to conform to His highest and most wonderful standards. Just as a newborn baby is not a member of his family on the basis of his conduct but on the basis of his inheritance, so, too, we are adopted into the family of God freely, not on the basis of our conduct but on the basis of adoption. However, as time goes by, the parents of the baby are going to expect him to live up to the family standards and to show forth character and behavior similar to that of the parents.

In the same way, God adopted us into His family when our behavior left much to be desired, but as time goes on He expects us to be able to show forth more and more of His character and a style of behavior that is more and more in keeping with His nature and His standards.

But how can we who are fallen human beings behave with the high standards of our holy God? It was precisely because we were unable to do this, that we needed God's forgiveness in the first place. If we failed to live up to His standards before we accepted His forgiveness, will we not fail equally now? The answer to this question would be "Yes" if God did no more for us than forgive our sins.

However, He offers us even more than forgiveness. He gives us the gift of a new heart of love to replace the old corrupted selfish heart. He literally offers us a spiritual heart transplant to replace the old failing spirit (heart) that was unable to function with the kind of character which God intends us to have. This new heart which God gives us is the same Spirit (heart) which moved Jesus and empowered Him to live as the perfect Son of God.

This amazing spiritual heart transplant was prophesied many years earlier by the prophet Jeremiah: *"Behold the days are coming, says the Lord, when I will make a new covenant with the house of Israel and with the house of Judah, not like the covenant which I made with their fathers when I took them by the hand to bring them out of the land of Egypt, my covenant which they broke, though I was their husband, says the Lord. But this is the covenant which I will make with the house of Israel after those days, says the Lord: I will put my law within them, and I will write it upon their hearts; and I will be their God, and they shall be my people. And no longer shall each man teach his neighbor, and each his brother, saying, 'Know the Lord,' for they shall all know me from the least of them to the greatest, says the Lord: for I will forgive their iniquity, and I will remember their sin no more"* (Jeremiah 31:31-34).

Just as it would be unrealistic to expect a man with a severely decayed heart to be able to perform all the activities of a healthy man, it would be unrealistic to expect men with decayed spiritual hearts to behave as men with perfect spiritual hearts. God's answer is to give us the spiritual heart transplant that was prophesied by the prophet Jeremiah.

It is only after He has removed our corrupted hearts and replaced them with a new perfect spiritual heart that He expects us to behave as spiritually healthy men and women. In Jesus, God offers every member of the race of Adam a spiritual heart transplant, and it is this new heart that can produce the kind of inner life that will bring forth in all of us the character and behavior God wants us to have.

Jesus put it this way: *"Are grapes gathered from thorns, or figs from thistles? So every sound tree bears good fruit, but the bad tree bears evil fruit. A sound tree cannot bear evil fruit nor can a bad tree bear good fruit. Every tree that does not bear good fruit is cut down and thrown into the fire. Thus you will know them by their fruits"* (Matthew 7:16-20).

The solution to the problem of our bad behavior as human beings is to replace the source of our wrong behavior with a perfect source. Jesus came not to IMPROVE our old natures but to replace them with His own. Everything that is, acts according to its nature. Cats behave like cats, dogs like dogs, giraffes like giraffes and humans like humans. We have inherited, by the ordinary laws of genetics, a nature that is self orientated and rebellious toward God. This was not the way man was originally made, but it is the way he has become since the primeval fall. That nature is passed on from parent to child.

God's purpose for man however, is that he bear the likeness of God in his nature, character and behavior. Since He can only act according to His nature, God's solution is thoroughly radical. He forgives man of the shortcomings of his old nature, and then replaces the old nature with a nature that is new, the nature of God Himself in human form. As man lives from the new nature, he will show forth the character of God in human form. It will be natural for him to act in a godly way.

On the earth today, there are two distinct species of human beings: those who have the nature of Adam and those who have the nature of God. All men are born "Adamians" (i.e. with the nature of Adam) but on the day God assumed a human nature, there appeared on the earth the first man who had a divine nature in human form.

On the day of the resurrection, this Man began to share His nature with all who would lay down their own Adam natures and receive of His Spirit. *"But to all who received him, who believed in his name, he gave power to become children of God; who were born, not of blood nor of the will of the flesh nor of the will of man, but of God"* (John 1:12-13).

John is announcing here that receiving the life of Jesus makes us children of God. Paul writes concerning the contrast between the old Adam nature and the new Christ nature in a way that makes clear the radical new beginning provided by this new nature, now available to all of us through Jesus.

"Thus it is written, 'The first man Adam became a living being'; the last Adam became a life-giving spirit. But it is not the spiritual which is first but the physical, and then the spiritual. The first man was from the earth, a man of dust; the second man is from heaven. As was the man of dust, so are those who are of the dust; and as is the man of heaven, so are those who are of heaven. Just as we have borne the image of the man of dust, we shall also bear the image of the man of heaven" (I Corinthians 15:45-49).

Every living thing behaves according to its nature and reproduces only that which has an identical nature to it. God's solution to the problems of our ungodly nature is to replace it with the divine-human nature which was in Jesus. He lays the axe to the root of our old nature and replaces it with the root system of His own life. *"Even now the axe is laid to the root of the trees; every tree therefore that does not bear good fruit is cut down and thrown into the fire"* (Matthew 3:10). Jesus gives the illustration to show that He has not come to reform our old natures but to cut them off and to replace them with the nature of His new life.

The real Christian life is not by any means a self-improvement course, though it has often been presented to us as if it were. It does not consist in an effort to improve, reform, or rehabilitate our old nature, but consists in a replacement of it by a new nature. As has often been said, it is not a CHANGED life but an EXCHANGED life; not a reformed life but a replaced life, which God gives us to live according to His ways.

Once upon a time there was a very ambitious crow. He wanted to be able to sing beautifully like a blackbird. He did not like the way he sang and he was determined not to remain like the rest of his relatives and ancestors.

He was going to become a great singer. He worked very hard, watched his diet carefully, exercised strenuously, studied diligently and practiced daily with all the determination it would take for him to become a great singer.

And so he applied himself to fulfill this great ambition. Years went by, hard years filled with long hours of study, practice and exercise, but in spite of all his effort and willingness, at the end of that time all that would come forth from his crow beak was a raucous "Caw! Caw!". With all of his music study and practice and training he could not significantly improve upon his singing. Indeed he had studied and read so much about music that he knew more about the subject than any bird alive, including the mellifluous blackbirds who did not even know how to read music.

The poor crow was greatly dejected. There never was a more determined bird, and yet it seemed that it was going to take something more than determination or will-power. He was frustrated.

One day as he was reading his morning newspaper, he read there about a famous surgeon who was able to perform the amazing surgical feat of transplanting voices. "This is what I need," he thought. "All my efforts up until now have not succeeded into making my voice sound like that of a blackbird. I will fly to the surgeon and ask him to give me a voice transplant, and to replace my crow's voice box with a blackbird's."

So he met with the distinguished surgeon. He was accepted for surgery. When the blackbird voice became available, the crow was operated upon and received a transplant of a blackbird's voice box to replace his own. In due time, after the healing had taken place and the surgical stitches removed, at last the crow could begin to try out his new voice. He began to sing, beautiful sweet notes, just like those of a blackbird. Just as it had been natural for him to sing like a crow before he had the operation, it was now perfectly natural for him to sing like a blackbird.

The new heart which we receive from Jesus is a spiritual transplant operation which replaces our old human heart with the Spirit of Jesus. This transplant is called the new birth. It is as natural for the new heart which Jesus gives us (which is His Spirit) to love as it was for our old heart to look out for its own interests and to be self centered. Jesus promised this new heart to those who would receive it. The prophets foresaw it, as we have seen, and finally on the day of the resurrection Jesus made this heart available to his disciples who were commissioned to announce to all men that this heart was available to as many as would receive it.

"Whoever drinks of the water that I shall give him will never thirst; the water that I shall give him will become in him a spring of water welling up to eternal life" (John 4:14).

"If any one thirst, let him come to me and drink. He who believes in me as the scripture has said, 'Out of his heart shall flow rivers of living water.' Now this he said about the Spirit, which those who believed in Him were to receive; for as yet the Spirit had not been given, because Jesus was not yet glorified" (John 7:37-39).

"On the evening of that day," (the day of Jesus' resurrection)...*"Jesus came and stood among them and said to them: 'Peace be with you.' When he had said this, he showed them his hands and his side. Then the disciples were glad when they saw the Lord. Jesus said to them again, 'Peace be with you. As the Father has sent me, even so I send you.' And when he had said this, he breathed on them and said to them, 'Receive the Holy*

Spirit. If you forgive the sins of any, they are forgiven; and if you retain the sins of any, they are retained" (John 20:19-22).

This Spirit which Jesus gives us is a replacement for our bankrupt old natures which He bore on the cross. We may receive forgiveness for the old as we have seen, but we can also lay it down on Jesus and replace it with the life of His Spirit. This becomes, as He promised, a river of life, righteousness, love and joy welling up within all who receive it. It is this the apostle spoke about when he wrote: *"If any one is in Christ, he is a new creation; the old has passed away, Behold the new has come. All this is from God, who through Christ reconciled us to himself and gave us the ministry of reconciliation"* (II Corinthians 5:17-18).

We would like to give one more example to illustrate the radical nature of this new life that Jesus gives us. Once there was a beautiful valley, nestled between the wooded peaks of a great mountain range. How beautiful the valley was and how unspoiled.

One day the head of a large paper company came to the valley and spoke with the people of the valley. He was aware of their economic problems and he wanted to help them. He also wanted to erect a factory in the heart of their valley which would make paper from wood pulp. At first, the people of the valley welcomed the idea. Their economy desperately needed an industry that would provide employment for the people and so they agreed to allow the factory to be built.

Time went by, and a few years after the factory had been in operation, the happiness of the valley people began to change to disappointment and even anger towards the new industrial plant. Since the factory had been in operation, the clear bright air of the valley had gradually been replaced by a gray sooty smog. Gone were the pristine scenic views, and on most days one could not even see the nearest mountains because of the sooty pall of smoke.

The county commissioner began to take action. He met with the factory executives and explained to them that the factory was violating their clean air standards. The factory owners pleaded for patience and forgiveness, explaining how difficult it was to operate a factory such as theirs without such waste, and still produce a profit. The county officials forgave them; however, there was still no improvement. Again and again the county officials complained to the factory executives and again and again the factory executives pleaded for patience and forgiveness. Again and again the county officials had patience with them and forgave them.

After some years the county officials began to realize that while the act of forgiveness did enable them to coexist with the factory owners and executives, it was doing nothing to remedy the situation. They came up with a costly, but effective solution. They collected money through a special tax and purchased a new smoke free power system for the factory. The old furnaces and chimneys were destroyed and replaced with new pollution-free energy system. Now the offending factory was not just forgiven but changed so that it was no longer an offense. Everybody was very happy.

This is exactly what God has done for us in Christ. He has forgiven the transgressions of our old nature and replaced our offending natures with the nature of His own Son.

"If anyone is in Christ, he is new creation, the old has passed away, behold the new has come" (II Corinthians 5:17).

A Prayer

Thank you, Father, for the gift of the new life of Jesus to become my life. May your life act through me and be expressed through me always.

CHAPTER 5

THE DOUBLE GIFT
OF THE HOLY SPIRIT

Jesus said that He came that we *"might have life and have it more abundantly"* (John 10:10). He came not only to be our Passover Lamb who would die for our sins, but to give us new life.

This new life comes to us in the person of the Holy Spirit. This is the new life that Jesus came to bring. He referred to the Holy Spirit as *the promise of the Father.* Jesus gives the Holy Spirit in two distinct and different ways. Firstly, as a new source of inner life, and secondly, as the Enabler and Anointing who leads us in the pattern and powerful ministry of Jesus. The first aspect of the gift of the Holy Spirit gives to us a share in the nature of Christ. The second aspect of the gift gives us a share in the ministry of Christ.

On the day that Jesus rose from the dead, He appeared to His disciples and breathed upon them and gave them the gift of the Holy Spirit to dwell within them. *"On the evening of that day, the first day of the week, the doors being shut where the disciples were, for fear of the*

Jews, Jesus came and stood among them and said to them, 'Peace be with you.' When he had said this he showed them His hands and His side. Then the disciples were glad when they saw the Lord. Jesus said to them again, 'Peace be with you.' As the Father sent me, even so I send you. And when He had said this, He breathed on them and said to them, 'Receive the Holy Spirit. If you forgive the sins of any they are forgiven; if you retain the sins of any, they are retained'" (John 20:19-23).

This *breathing* by Jesus on His disciples reminds us of the time when God created man out of the dust of the earth. He *breathed* on it and formed man from it. Now Jesus breathes a *new life* into earthly man, a life that Adam never had even before the fall. It is a share in His own resurrection life that Jesus is imparting to be the life of those who will receive it.

The Spirit that was present in Jesus and raised Him from the dead then comes into us to be the Spirit which moves our lives and makes us spiritually alive. *"The Spirit who raised Jesus from the dead will give life to your mortal bodies also through his Spirit which dwells in you"* (Romans 8:11). *"The first man Adam became a living being; the last Adam became a life-giving spirit"* (I Corinthians 15:45).

When Jesus breathed on His disciples on that great day, they received into their innermost beings the very life that was in Him. This life was given to be the motivating influence of their lives forever. Up until this time man was controlled by his soul (his mind, intellect and emotions). Now he could be motivated by the living Spirit and Life of God Himself. *"He who is united with the Lord becomes one spirit with Him"* (I Corinthians 6:17).

When anyone becomes born of the Spirit of Jesus, he

receives into himself the very life that was in Jesus, and so he can begin to reproduce the nature of Jesus. The life that was in Jesus can now come forth through others also. Jesus came to be *the first of many brothers.* The rivers of love and kindness and godliness that were expressed through Jesus can now be expressed through many others.

He said, *"Whoever drinks of the water that I shall give him will never thirst; the water that I shall give him shall become in him a spring of water welling up to eternal life"* (John 4:14). It was on the day of His resurrection that men first drank of this eternal river of life.

After they had received this new life from Jesus, they rejoiced in it and for forty days Jesus explained to them more fully what it meant. Finally, the day came when Jesus was to depart from the earth, at least in the visible sense. (He has continued to remain on the earth in the invisible but real realm of the spirit.)

The time had now come when the disciples would be called into every corner of the earth to proclaim the reconciliation that God had accomplished through Jesus and to invite all men to receive for themselves the Holy Spirit. To perform this task would take not only great courage and boldness, but great love and the powerful presence of God Himself.

Jesus promised them, however, that He would send the Holy Spirit in a new way to come upon them to guide them and equip them. His presence with them would confirm their message with healing signs and wonders. As He was departing, He said to them: *"And behold, I send the promise of the Father upon you; but stay in the city until you are clothed with power from on high"* (Luke 24:49). *"But you shall receive power when the Holy Spirit has come upon you; and you shall be my wit-*

nesses in Jerusalem, and in all Judea, and Samaria and to the end of the earth" (Acts 1:8).

Within a few days, the Holy Spirit did come upon them in a spectacular way and from that moment they were empowered to proclaim the gospel in strength. They were launched on a life that would be lived out in the obedient pattern of Jesus.

When Jesus told His disciples that they should *wait* in the city until the Holy Spirit would come upon them and clothe them *with power from on high,* they had already received the Holy Spirit WITHIN them. (On the day when Jesus rose, they had been born from above and had received the life of God's Spirit WITHIN them.) To do the works that He had called them to do, they would need the Holy Spirit to also come UPON them.

Just as Jesus Himself was filled with the Holy Spirit for thirty years before the Holy Spirit came upon Him to anoint Him for His powerful mission, so too the disciples were filled with the Holy Spirit for forty days before they received the power of the Holy Spirit UPON them to anoint them for their mission.

The new birth is a *drink of living water.* It happens whenever anyone receives the Holy Spirit to fill their innermost beings. When one is baptized with the Holy Spirit, the Holy Spirit comes ON the person to anoint that person to be an effective and powerful witness for Christ and His kingdom.

(When one drinks a glass of water, one gets wet on the inside, but remains dry on the outside. When one gets baptized in water, on the other hand, one remains dry on the inside, but gets wet on the outside. Obviously, the two contacts with water are quite different.)

The Holy Spirit comes INTO us when Jesus gives us a *drink of living water.* At that point we receive a *drink* of

His Spirit and receive a New Life WITHIN us. When Jesus BAPTIZES us with the Holy Spirit, on the other hand, He causes us to be surrounded with the presence and power of the Holy Spirit who comes UPON us through this baptism. It is not hard for anyone to see that there is an enormous difference between a drink and an immersion or baptism. Jesus gives us first a drink of His Spirit and then an immersion into that Spirit.

In the Old Testament days, no one had yet received the Holy Spirit within them. This could not happen until the day of Jesus' resurrection. However, in the Old Testament days the Holy Spirit was very active and it was He who came UPON the prophets, priests and kings to equip them for their offices. In those days the Holy Spirit could come UPON people to anoint them for a task but could not come WITHIN any of them. That is why John says in his gospel when he talks about the period prior to Jesus' death and resurrection: *as yet the Spirit had not been given because Jesus was not yet glorified*" (John 7:39).

He writes, "*On the last day of the feast, the great day, Jesus stood up and proclaimed: 'If any man thirst let him come to me and drink. He who believes in me, as the scripture has said, Out of his heart shall flow rivers of living water.' Now this He said about the Spirit which those who believed in Him were to receive; for as yet the Spirit had not been given because Jesus was not yet glorified*" (John 7:37-39).

It was only after Jesus' death, resurrection and glorification that the Holy Spirit could be given to us to come within us as a new principle of life. Our old fallen natures had first to be borne by Jesus to the cross before they could be replaced by the new nature.

As we have seen, it was those who had drunk of the Spirit on the day of Jesus' resurrection who went to the upper room to await the Baptism with the Holy Spirit which they received on the day of Pentecost.

All believers in Jesus are offered New Life by Him. If they accept what He offers, they receive the Holy Spirit WITHIN them. After that they are offered a share in Jesus' anointing through the Baptism with the Holy Spirit which is a pouring out of the Holy Spirit upon them. Believers must receive the New Life of Jesus WITHIN them, and then they may present themselves to fulfill Jesus' mission and receive the Baptism with the Holy Spirit, the Spirit UPON them.

And so we see that Jesus gives the Holy Spirit to all who will receive from Him in two separate ways: firstly, as the life of the Holy Spirit to be a river of pure water flowing from within our innermost beings, and secondly, as the supernatural Equipper and Presence who enables us to be bold Christian witnesses and obedient servants. The first is the Resurrection gift of the Holy Spirit, and the second is the Pentecost gift of the Holy Spirit. The first giving of the Spirit reproduces the character of Christ in us and the second produces a share in the ministry and obedient service of Jesus in us.

Most of the things of the Spirit are beyond the reach of our minds. The Holy Spirit enables us to pray (if we cooperate with Him) in a language that reaches beyond the limits of our minds. *"Likewise the Spirit helps us in our weakness; for we do not know how to pray as we ought, but the Spirit himself intercedes for us with sighs too deep for words. And he who searches the hearts of men knows what is the mind of the Spirit because the Spirit intercedes for the saints according to the will of God"* (Romans 8:26-27).

This gift and various other manifestations of the Spirit will evidence themselves in the lives of all believers who ask Jesus to anoint them with His Spirit, and who then actively receive the Holy Spirit and willingly pray in tongues as the Spirit gives them the ability. We do the praying and the Holy Spirit makes it a language of deep communication to God. It is not automatic. The person must begin to speak words in a language he does not understand and the Holy Spirit makes it a language understood by the Father. In this way, we are enabled to pray in a way that is deeper than our understanding.

"For one who speaks in a tongue, speaks not to men but to God; for no one understands him but he utters mysteries in the Spirit. On the other hand, he who prophesies speaks to men for their upbuilding and encouragement and consolation. He who speaks in a tongue edifies himself, but he who prophesies edifies the church. Now I want you all to speak in tongues but even more to prophesy" (I Corinthians 14:2-5).

Have you received both aspects of Jesus' gift of the Holy Spirit, the drink of living water to fill your heart with the life of Jesus as well as the pouring out of the Spirit to anoint you to the service and and self-emptying of Jesus?

A Prayer

Jesus, I thank you for bearing my sins on yourself and for filling me with the New Life of Your Spirit. Thank you for that drink of living water. I now present my life to You so that You can use me as a channel of Your love, truth and healing. I ask you now to baptize me with the Holy Spirit and with power that I may serve You, not in my power but in the power of the Spirit and I will speak in tongues right now as You give me the ability. I am Yours. Send me. Use me.

Amen.

CHAPTER 6

CHOSEN FOR GOOD WORKS

There once was an ambitious student who went to college and studied diligently to get a degree. Upon successfully completing his studies, he graduated and became the proud bearer of a degree. From then on he went into retirement and lived an idle life off his father's fortune.

We quickly see something very inconsistent and incongruous about such a quest for a college education. We know that the degree and the education is not to be a badge of honor but an equipping for work. Today many Christians rejoice that they have been born from above, restored into right relationship with God, baptized with the Holy Spirit and endued with the power of God, and yet they produce little fruit.

God loves us and accepts us not on the basis of our works or for our conduct. He simply accepts and forgives us. However, as we have seen, He then begins to change us and to equip us to fulfill various missions and works He has appointed for us. It is very important that we see that these works are not the condition for getting into fellowship with God but are simply the fruit of this new relationship. *"For we are his workmanship, created in Christ Jesus for good works, which God prepared beforehand that we should walk in them"* (Ephesians 2:10). He has chosen us *for* works, not *because of* works.

These works are not the works we would choose for ourselves in our own planning or ambition, but they are works God has chosen for us. Neither are they the works which our families or culture might expect of us. These works are works for which God has appointed us and for which he personally chooses and equips us.

It is a travesty, therefore, for any religious group or personage to usurp this call of God on a person's life and to take on themselves the role of God by projecting on a person works to which God has not appointed that person.

Good Christian fellowship and pastoral care can, of course, be a tremendous help to us when we are seeking to discern God's call on our lives. The role of the pastoral ministry in the church in such cases is to assist the person, discern their call and help them find the outlets to fulfill those works to which they believe the Lord is calling them.

The role of the pastoral office is never, or ought never to be, to substitute man chosen activity, even if it is religious activity, for works which God wishes to unfold in the life of a disciple.

Of course, at times, God's appointed works for us may coincide with a religious program or a social demand, but frequently His plans will not coincide with these. Every disciple will discover this. We must be continually working to be like Jesus, doing only those things which the Father wants us to do and desisting from every activity to which He does not appoint us.

"I can do nothing on my own authority," says Jesus, *"As I hear, I judge; and my judgement is just, because I seek not my own will but the will of him who sent me"* (John 5:30).

In the life of the disciple there is a double process which takes place simultaneously. On the one hand there is a ceasing from our works and on the other there is a coming alive to those works which God would do through us. If we attempt to do God's works without desisting from our own works we will have a confused Christianity that will really fall short of full Christianity. Real Christianity is God at work in and through man and not so much man working for God.

When we cease from our own works, we make a great act of humility before God. To cease from our own works does not mean we are henceforth to retire from all works and live a life of idleness. Some of God's children have done this. God wants us to cease from our own works, that is, to cease from those activities which have their origin in us and to give ourselves over to those works He may wish to do with us and through us.

We are to cease from our own works and make ourselves available for those works He wants to do through us. *"I appeal to you therefore, brethren, by the mercies of God, to present your bodies as a living sacrifice, holy and acceptable to God which is your spiritual worship"* (Romans 12:1).

Paul is urging his readers not to stop at the point of coming to an end of self and the works of the self, but to respond, come alive and make themselves available as living sacrifices for the works God would do through them.

God's Rest and Ours

Jesus said: *"Come to me, all who labor and are heavy laden, and I will give you rest. Take my yoke upon you and learn from me; for I am gentle and lowly in heart, and you will find rest for your souls. For my yoke is easy and my burden is light"* (Matthew 11:28-30). In Hebrews it is written: *"So then there remains a sabbath rest for the people of God; for whoever enters God's rest also ceases from his labors as God did from His"* (Hebrews 4:9-10).

The man of faith rests on what Jesus has wrought through His death, resurrection and ascension. He knows that since he has been graciously united to Christ in His death and with Him in His resurrection and ascension, he is now in spirit *seated together with Him in heavenly places.* He is not *trying* to get there any more than he would try to get into the air he breathes.

A man who is under the water may struggle to reach the air, but a man who is on dry land does not struggle to reach the air for he is already in it. So, too, the man who is not in right fellowship with God may struggle to get there, but the man who has been lifted into fellowship with God and into the realm of His kingdom no longer needs to struggle to get there.

So many Christians labor so hard trying to get closer and closer to God as if closeness to God were some zenith to be achieved with just a little more prayer, another revelation or more commitment.

Jesus, by identifying us in Himself, has already brought us nigh to God the Father. Positionally, we are as close to God as we can possibly be. We cannot be made any closer to Him. There is a rest then for us when we see this truth. Since our position is in Christ, we cannot get closer than that. We can rest in this position and enjoy it all of our lives provided we abide in Christ. What a tremendous rest this is for the people of God!

The long, long effort to climb the tedious and often cruel ladder of religion has come to an end for us who have been mercifully lifted up to be *in Christ* who sits at the right hand of the Father.

We hope you are not trying to work to get into this wonderful position; for if you are, it will just wear you out. We who have believed have entered into a rest and have been brought by Jesus to a place which we could never attain by our own efforts even if we were to groan and sweat all the days of our lives. Once having been brought to this position, it is useless to try to expend energy to get there. You are already there.

If this is the case, is there any place for works left in the Christian life? No, there is not, for those aspects of adoption which have been established for us by Jesus can only be entered into by faith.

At the same time we can say yes, there is a very important place for works in the Christian life both because faith itself includes a certain action and corresponding action and because after we have been adopted and lifted into union with Jesus in His death, resurrection and ascension, He sends us into the world to fulfill a mission which certainly includes works.

After Jesus had risen and ascended to the Father, He appeared to His disciples and said: *"Peace be with you. As the Father has sent me, even so I send you"* (John 20:21). Having identified us with Himself in His own death, resurrection and ascension, He now sends us into the world in exactly the manner in which the Father had sent Him into the world. We are sent into the world from the realm of the ascension, from the realm of our union to fulfill a mission, to do the works He gives us to do.

We work, then, not to *attain* our union with Him but FROM that union we work with Him. From this place of union we go forth into the world to do many good works for which He appoints us. These good works are not our own works but works He does through us, works that are the products of this union.

Sometimes Christians like to stop at the point of union. We must move now into the world in a way that keeps us always in union with Him and our position with Him in the heavenlies. We move to witness to this reconciliation that He has established by His death, resurrection and ascension and to respond in action to those works He sends us to perform. We are now moved from within as Jesus was moved.

We are no longer moved by mere social convention or social pressure. We refuse to be moved by the nervous energy of our own flesh or by the lusts of the flesh. We are moved now by the Holy Spirit. *"For all who are led by the Spirit of God are the sons of God"* (Romans 8:14).

We are moved by compassion, the selfless selfgiving love that is inspired, not by sentiment, but by the very heart of God in us. This compassion moves us to work in the service in the tasks to which God appoints us with a selfless and tireless zeal. *"For the love of Christ controls us,"* Paul writes, *"because we are convinced that one has died for all; therefore all have died. And he died for all, that those who live might live no longer for themselves but for Him who for their sake died and was raised"* (2 Corinthians 5:14,15).

God is calling us not only to die in Christ but to come alive in Him and to go forth into the world to do those works which He calls us to. *"So you also must consider yourselves dead to sin and alive to God in Christ Jesus"* (Romans 6:11).

He is calling us away from the religious activity in which we may engage to establish a relationship with God. He is calling us to accept a relationship with Him established through His mercy and not through our works. He is calling us away from a life of slavery to works imposed on us by fear, flesh or religious practitioners.

He is calling us FROM all these works TO works chosen by Him. He wants us to go into the world from the position of heavenly union and be obedient to those works and missions to which He appoints us.

John, the beloved disciple, humble man that he was, writes: *"As he is so are we in this world"* (I John 4:17). When we become united with Him in His death, resurrection and ascension by faith by putting off the old self and the ways of the old self, we are to go into the world from this heavenly position. Our relationship with the world is now totally new and different than what it was before we came into this glorious union. We are no longer living FROM the world, though we are living IN the world. We have been linked up to the supply line of heaven even though we live on earth. We are in the world but not of it.

"If the world hates you, know that it has hated me before it hated you. If you were of the world, the world would love its own; but because you are not of the world, but I chose you out of the world, therefore the world hates you," says Jesus (John 15:18-19).

Jesus is sending us into the world as the Father sent Him. He did not go into the world to condemn the world but to save the world and to witness the truth to the people of the world. As we go into the world, we go in the same relationship with the Father as Jesus has always had and which He had as a man. (The relationship He has with the Father by His very nature, He *gives* to us as we abide in Him, so that we receive by union and by grace what is His by nature.)

Everything we have, we have in Him and through Him. How tremendous the call to be in the world with the same relationship with God our Father as Jesus had as He walked on earth as a man. Going into the world from this position means that we not only have Jesus' relationship with His Father, but His relationship with the world and with the devil. We are not to be afraid because the resources of heaven are committed to us as we seek to abide in Christ. John writes, *"He who is in you is greater than he who is in the world"* (I John 4:4).

Knowing this relationship, it remains for us to act according to this relationship and, like Jesus, to accomplish the work which God has given us to do, so that we may be able to say one day, as Jesus said: *"Father, I glorified thee on earth, having accomplished the work which thou gavest me to do"* (John 17:4).

In this manner let us go forth into the world to fulfill our days, eager to find and do those works He has sent us to accomplish in, through and with Him. Let us go from a position of rest and union with God through Jesus as we eagerly await and anticipate the manifestation of His Glory ready to be revealed.

"The Glory that the Father has given me,
I have given to them."
(John 17:22)

"Even so, Come Lord Jesus!"
(Revelation 22:20)

Part II
THE WAY - LED BY THE SPIRIT

CHAPTER 7

FREEDOM IN THE SPIRIT

"There is therefore now no condemnation for those who are in Christ Jesus. For the law of the spirit of life in Christ Jesus has set me free from the law of sin and death. For God has done what the law, weakened by the flesh, could not do. Sending his own Son in the likeness of sinful flesh and for sin, he condemned sin in the flesh, in order that the just requirement of the law might be fulfilled in us who walk not according to the flesh but according to the Spirit" (Romans 8:1-4).

There is, through the work of Jesus on the cross for all who believe, freedom from guilt and condemnation, freedom from sin and freedom from the law. In Romans, chapter six, seven and eight, Paul explains to his readers how they have been set free from the law when they chose to live in the Spirit.

This truth is often misunderstood by Christians. They wonder how God could set us free from the law of Moses with its rules and regulations. They think that it would be dangerous to teach people that when they come into Christ, they are truly free from the law. They fear that if this were preached that people would live very lax lives. For this reason many prefer to teach that we must still keep new and old laws to maintain a right standing with God.

While scarcely any Christians will teach that we must keep the whole law that God gave to Moses, many, if not most, teach that we must keep a modified version of the Mosaic law as interpreted by their particular denomination.

In the first two verses of Romans 8 that we have quoted above, there are three laws referred to: first, the law of the spirit of life, second, the law of sin and death, and third, the law of Moses. *"The law of the Spirit of life in Christ Jesus has set me free from the law of sin and death"* (Romans 8:2). As it was and is, the law of Moses could never accomplish what the law of the spirit of life can do in believers' lives.

All men who came into this world since the time of Adam have been subject to the law of sin and death. This law pulls at everyone of us to drag us toward destruction. This law even pulls at born again Christians. However they have within them a power that is stronger than that negative force of sin and death.

The law of sin and death is rather like the law of gravity which holds everyone of us down to the earth. The only way for us to escape the earth's gravitational pull is by putting into operation other laws which would be stronger and more powerful than the law of gravity.

We now know, of course, that there are indeed laws that we can exploit which are stronger than the laws of gravity. These are the laws of aerodynamics. When a great airplane takes off from a runway, it escapes the pull of gravity by putting into operation laws of aerodynamics. By exploiting these laws the airplane is able to get free from the law of gravity. The law of gravity is still there but as long as the engines of the jet are exploiting the laws of aerodynamics, the airplane is able to fly free from the pull of gravity.

This is a parallel of what God does for us when He places within us the resurrection life of Jesus. This life in us is like the law of aerodynamics which enables the giant airplane to escape the law of gravity. As long as the engines are functioning and running, the airplane can remain free from the law of gravity; however, should they be cut off, then, of course, the airplane will fall. As long as we remain in tune with the resurrection life of Christ in us, we remain free from the law of sin and death; but should we let go of our union with Christ, we will fall back under the control of sin.

Until the laws of aerodynamics were discovered and man learned to build machines that would exploit those laws, it was impossible for man to fly. In a similar way, it was impossible for man to get free from the law of sin and death until Jesus gave His life to dwell within us. Until that time the law that God gave to Moses for the people of Israel restrained them, though it did not free them from the law of sin and death. It had, however, no power to set anyone free from that law.

An Illustration

Some time ago we watched on T.V. the space shuttle being launched from the Kennedy Space center in Florida. Several days before the launch, the spacecraft was taken out and set in position for launching. The space shuttle was secured to the vertical platform by means of several bolts and fasteners to hold the shuttle in place. Should they be removed before the rocket engines are fired, the shuttle would be in great danger of falling over, knocked down by the wind or pulled down by the force of gravity.

The space shuttle has a destiny to fulfill...to get free from the force of gravity's powers which could pull it to the ground. In the days before the launch, this spacecraft stands clumsily, prevented from the destructive power of gravity only by the launching platform to which it is secured. It needs those securing bolts if it is to avoid being toppled over and shattered on the ground.

Finally, the great day of the launch arrives. The countdown is almost complete and the rockets are ignited. A tremendous surge of power is released within the engines of the launching rockets and the spacecraft begins to rise in a great explosion of power headed to its destination in the heavens. As it rises, it separates from the launching platform and rises above the gravitational pull of the earth.

Occasionally, when the engineers wish to test the rocket system of the spacecraft before launching, they will fire the rockets but prevent the spacecraft from taking off by keeping it secured to the launching pad. Until the rockets are ignited, the launching pad, platform and securing bolts are the only things that keep the spacecraft from being pulled to the ground.

However, after the rocket engines have been ignited, the security bolts will be a hindrance to the launching of the rocket if the spacecraft continues to remain tied to them. That which had previously been an aid to the spacecraft in its 'struggle' against gravity will now be a hindrance to it.

This illustration shows how the law given to Moses along with other religious laws must be left behind by all who accept the life of Jesus as the driving force of their lives. Just as the launching pad and the bolts were the first stage in the spacecrafts' efforts to get free of the law of gravity, so the law of Moses, and any other similar religious and moral laws, are important first steps in restraining us from the law of sin and death.

Paul says, *"Now before faith came, we were confined under the law, kept under restraint until faith should be revealed. So that the law was our custodian until Christ came that we might be justified by faith. But now that faith has come, we are no longer under a custodian"* (Galatians 3:23-25).

Thousands of Jewish people in the time of the first apostles and in every subsequent generation, have seen these truths and have entered into a true and full appropriation of the essence of their Jewish heritage. They see that the law was a preparation period for the day of the Messiah and the day when God would write His law within the hearts of all who would come to Him. However, in every generation since Christ, some Christians and Jews have tried to hold on to the Mosaic law and still follow Jesus the Messiah, or have tried to follow Jesus with a modified or reformed version of the law.

The scriptures absolutely forbid anyone from adding or subtracting from the words of the law. Jesus Himself was most adamant on this point: *"For truly, I say unto you, till heaven and earth pass away not an iota, not a dot will pass from the law until all is accomplished"* (Matthew 5:18).

Jesus did not come to destroy the law, but to fulfill it and bring us into a higher realm of righteousness than that which could be attained through the law. *"For I tell you, unless your righteousness exceeds that of the scribes and Pharisees, you will never enter into the kingdom of heaven"* (Matthew 5:20).

To return to our illustration, the spacecraft will never get into the heavens unless it goes higher and further than the bolts on the launching pad platform would permit. To get free to go with its powerful rocket engines, the shuttle must leave the props at the launching pad. The space shuttle does not destroy the launching pad. It simply rises above it fulfilling its intended purpose. The shuttle leaves the bolts intact, but leaves them behind as it becomes subject to a different law.

Illustration II - The Greasy Pole

The following is another way we can clarify our relationship to the law of the spirit of life in Christ Jesus, the law of sin and death and the law of Moses. The illustration is perhaps a little far-fetched but the point it clearly makes is vitally important.

Imagine a man who tried to get free of the pull of gravity by trying to climb a tall, greasy pole. It was a tremendous struggle for him to keep from slipping. Indeed, he found that the faster he climbed, the more he slipped. The pole did prevent him from falling into the mud beneath, but he was not able to make any upward progress.

After some time, someone came by and attached a great helium balloon to his shoulders. As soon as the balloon was attached, he was now able to let go of the pole without risk of falling into the mud beneath. However, the man was afraid to let go of the pole because he was not quite sure that the balloon would hold him up.

Before the balloon had been attached, the pole was the only thing that stood between him and the mud. It had been his only means of escape; thus, it was difficult for him to release his desperate grip on that pole. As long as he continued to clutch on to that pole, the balloon could not lift him. The pole which had been a help to him in his effort to get clear of the mud was holding him back. Before the balloon was attached, it would have been disastrous to let go of the pole; however now that the balloon was connected to him, the pole ceased to be a help and had become instead a hindrance to his progress.

Some distance away stood an observer. He had watched the desperate strugglings of the man on the pole. He had watched when the balloon had been fixed to the man's shoulders. He had watched the man continue to clutch on to the pole fearful of letting go.

The observer took a gun from his pocket, aimed in the direction of the man on the pole and shot. The bullet hit the man killing him instantly. Falling dead, the man released his grip on the pole. However, he did not fall to the ground. As he slumped dead, the balloon carried him up and away into the skies.

This tale illustrates some important truths concerning our relationship with the law of sin and death (which in the story corresponds to the law of gravity), the law of Moses and the laws of religious traditions and ordinances (which are represented in the story by the pole), and the law of the spirit of life in Christ Jesus (which is represented in the story by the balloon).

Both the pole and the balloon had a common purpose which was to keep the man free from the mud towards which he was being pulled by the law of gravity. The pole did not have sufficient power to protect him from the pull of gravity. When the balloon was attached, it was not able to lift him until his hands let go of the pole.

In a similar way, when the resurrection life of Jesus comes into us and we flow with it, we have within us a new principle of incorruptible life which is greater than the pull of sin and death. However, if we are still trying to escape sin by means of keeping laws, rules and regulations, the life of Jesus cannot carry us.

In the letter to the Galatians, Paul says that if, after the life of Christ has come into us, we go back to the law (remain holding on to our greasy poles) Christ will be of no avail to us. Just as the balloon cannot carry us as long as we clutch on to the pole, so Christ cannot carry us as long as we remain attached to the law as our means of spiritual progress.

"You are severed from Christ," he writes, *"you who would be justified by the law; you have fallen away from grace"* (Galatians 5:4).

These Galatian Christians, most of whom were Jewish, experienced tremendous blessings and miracles when they were first converted. They lost that early sense of blessing and the demonstration of God's presence among them disappeared. Paul attributed their loss of blessing to their attempt to hold on to the law and to Christ at the same time.

To keep holding on to the old law while they tried to follow Christ only negated and neutralized their connection with Christ. They were still attached to Christ, but they had bound up His presence in them. *"If justification were through the law, then Christ died to no purpose,"* he writes in Galatians 2:21.

The experience of those Galatian Christians has been repeated in the lives of thousands of church groups. Beginning with simple faith in the mercy of God, they experience abundant evidence of His blessings and goodness. Then they seek to maintain their union with God through laws instead of through simple, ongoing dependance on Christ.

The law had its purpose for a set time as a restraining and convicting force; but when Christ, who is the fulfillment of the law, comes, then the hour of the law is finished.

(It is important to note here that though the hour of the law is finished as soon as one turns to Christ, God still has a unique purpose for the Jewish people. He called them over four hundred years before the law was given. That call exists for all generations even after the law has become obsolete. When we say, as the writer of the letter to the Hebrews says, that the law is not obsolete, we are not saying that God's covenant with and call on the Jewish people is obsolete. The covenant and call both supersede and precede the law that was given through Moses.)

Many believers are under the mistaken impression that the life of Christ is given to us to enable us to keep the law. This is a mistaken impression. The early Christians, even those who were Jewish did not keep the law all of the time. *"If you, though a Jew, live like a Gentile and not like a Jew, how can you compel the Gentiles to live like Jews?"* Paul wrote in his letter to the Galatians (Galatians 2:14). He was pointing out that Peter, one of the greatest Jewish leaders of the church, did not consistently obey the law. *"The law was our custodian until Christ came that we might be justified by faith. But now that faith has come, we are no longer under a custodian; for in Christ Jesus you are all sons of God through faith"* (Galatians 3:24-26).

The law has not changed, nor can it ever be changed, but we have been taken away from its custody. Through Moses, God placed the Jewish people under the custody of the law, but in Jesus, He wants to remove them from the law and to place them under Jesus' custody. John writes: *"For the law was given through Moses; grace and truth came through Jesus Christ"* (John 1:17).

Just as the man on the pole could make no more progress after the balloon was attached to him until he let go of the pole to go with the balloon, so today many believers cannot progress in the Spirit until they are willing to be obedient to the leading of the Holy Spirit and the teachings of Jesus above every other law in their lives.

God is calling His people to perfection, but we cannot move on towards that perfection as long as we substitute the leading of the law for the leading of the Holy Spirit. *"On the one hand, a former commandment is set aside because of its weakness and uselessness (for the law made nothing perfect); on the other hand, a better hope is introduced, through which we draw near to God"* (Hebrews 7:18-19).

Now the law is good, and has a purpose in God's dealing with us, but it is, as Hebrews says, *"But a shadow of the good things to come instead of the true form of these realities"* (Hebrews 10:1). Jesus has brought in a whole new order of reality in our relationship with God, and by His sacrifice, He has also brought in a new and eternal priesthood in which He is both eternal priest and eternal sacrifice.

The writer of Hebrews points out that *"When there is a change of priesthood, there is necessarily a change in the law as well"* (Hebrew 7:12). Jesus' death fulfills the requirements of the old law and inaugurates a new law — the law of the spirit of life in Christ Jesus. If believers are to put their faith in the eternal priestly work of Jesus, then they must come under His new law which exceeds the old law, and leave the old law.

"But as it is, Christ has obtained a ministry which is more excellant than the old just as the covenant He mediates is better, since it is enacted on better promises.

For if the first covenant had been faultless, there would have been no occasion for a second" (Hebrews 8:6-7).

"He finds fault with them when he says: 'The days will come, says the Lord, when I will establish a new covenant with the house of Israel and the house of Judah;... In speaking of a new covenant he treats the first as obsolete. And what is becoming obsolete and growing old is ready to vanish away'"(Hebrews 8:8,13). Many believers are afraid to let go of that which is obsolete. They must do so if they are to go on to perfection.

In saying that we have been released from the law of Moses we do NOT say that we have been released from obedience to God. Some believers have mistakenly understood their freedom from the old law as a freedom from ALL law. This, of course, is not the case. There is only one thing that can free us from the LAW of sin and death, and that is the LAW of the spirit of life in Christ Jesus. A new law has come to replace the old law. This new law is the law of the life of Christ Jesus in us. It is not an external law or code, but it is a law of life that is imparted to us.

This new life does not empower us to keep the old law but empowers us to keep and fulfill the new law. This new law is not a written code but a law, a life of selfless love which is infused into us by the Holy Spirit. The believers' responsibility is to remain attuned to the love, kindness and selflessness which this life of the Spirit causes to arise within the heart of every Christian. Just as the man attached to the balloon would fall instantly to the mud were he to let go of the balloon, so we who cleave to Christ have been freed from our various poles to cleave to Him and to do only those things which are in harmony with the righteous life He has infused into us.

The move from obedience to law to obedience to

Christ can be compared to a wedding. On the day of her wedding the bride moves from her father's care to her husband's care. During her childhood and adolescence she was in the care of her father and owed him her obedience.

On her wedding day she moves away from her dependency on her father and is released from any obedience to him. From now on she will work out her life in relationship with her husband. She will, of course, always honor and respect her father, but she is no longer required to give him her obedience.

In fact, it would be quite damaging to her relationship with her husband if she sought to obey her father as well as her husband. When she married, she was expected to leave her father and mother and to cleave to her husband.

In a similar way, when a person enters into union with Christ, he must leave the law (as good and wonderful as it is) and cleave to Him. If this does not take place, the union will never become strong. This does not mean that Jewish believers in Christ should leave behind their Jewish culture or their Jewishness, but they should lay aside any adherence to the law and traditions as their means of getting and staying close to God and as their principle of guidance.

In this discussion of the Christian's relationship with the law, no criticism of the law is intended, no more than the bride's departure from her parents to unite with her husband would constitute a criticism of them. Obedience to her parents has prepared her for her new life with her husband.

In a similar way the Jew's relationship with the law was intended as a temporary arrangement to prepare them for obedience to Christ through His implanted Spirit. The religious laws which many of us have grown up with in church can have a similar purpose in our lives inasmuch as they prepare us for obedience to Christ in the Spirit.

In Romans, Chapter 7, Paul explains that we have been freed from the law so that we can follow Jesus. He compares it to a woman being released from a difficult marriage so that she can marry the man of her heart. Under the law, there is no way out of this marriage except by the death of one of the spouses. The only way out for this unhappy lady is for her husband to die or for her to die. Paul goes on to explain that since we died in Christ, we have been discharged from the law because the law is binding on a person only during his life.

Christians have died in Christ and begin a brand new life through His Spirit. Being freed from the law and discharged from its obligations, we are free to be led by the loving Spirit of Jesus our Messiah. *"Likewise, my brethren, you have died to the law through the Body of Christ so that you may belong to another, to him who has been raised from the dead in order that we may bear fruit for God...But now we are DISCHARGED FROM THE LAW, dead to that which held us captive so that we serve not under the old written code but in the new life of the Spirit"* (Romans 7:4, 6).

Only through death can we be discharged from the old law. Since we died in Christ, we have been released from the law which had been given to govern and restrain the natural life we received from our father Adam. When we come to Christ, we lay down that life at the cross of Jesus and accept the new life of the Spirit. The new Christ-life is not governed by the law of Moses but by the laws and life of the Spirit. Moses' law was for fallen Adamic life, Jesus' law is for the new creation life.

Jesus' life is for those who have come to an end of the efforts of self-justification of the Adamic man and for those who have repented of working in their old energies and released themselves to work in and respond to the new life of the Spirit.

The balloon in our illustration could only carry the man after he had ceased his own efforts to escape the pull of gravity. After he had died, the balloon had no resistance and could carry him easily. We should be dead to the stirrings and strugglings of our own desperate efforts and alive to the promptings and leading of the Spirit of life in us. *"So you also must consider yourselves dead to sin and ALIVE to God in Christ Jesus"* (Romans 6:11).

The truths that we have been explaining here were explained by Jesus to His disciples in a different fashion on the day He took Peter, James and John with Him for prayer on Mount Tabor. *"And behold there appeared to them Moses and Elijah talking with him. And Peter said to Jesus: 'Lord, it is well that we are here; if you wish, I will make three booths here, one for you and one for Moses and one for Elijah.' He was still speaking when, lo, a bright cloud overshadowed them, and a voice from the cloud said, 'This is my beloved Son with whom I am well pleased; listen to him.' When the disciples heard this, they fell on their faces, and were filled with awe. But Jesus came and touched them, saying, 'Rise, and have no fear.' And when they lifted up their eyes, they saw no one but Jesus only. And as they were coming down the mountain, Jesus commanded them, 'Tell no one the vision, until the Son of man is raised from the dead'"* Matthew 17:3-9).

When Peter saw Moses and Elijah talking together with Jesus, he was pleased that Jesus was in such illustrious company and wanted to build a booth for each of them. The voice of God was heard commanding them to hear and obey Jesus and when they looked up again, they saw only Jesus.

Peter wanted to have Jesus with Moses and Elijah. Moses and Elijah represent the law and the prophets and Peter's desire to build a booth for each symbolizes his desire to have Jesus and the law. The fact that Moses and Elijah faded and God's voice commanded obedience to Jesus indicates that Moses and Elijah were receding to be replaced by Jesus.

Jesus commanded them not to report the vision until after the resurrection because the hour of discharge from the law of Moses was not until Jesus had paid the penalty for all of our transgressions under the law. By dying for us, He included us in His death so that we could be discharged from the law to receive the new life of the Spirit and obey Jesus. Moses and Elijah had fulfilled their mission and now the kingdom of God was at hand.

In this realm it is the new law of the spirit of life in Christ Jesus working together with the commands of Jesus that must be obeyed.

A PRAYER

Lord Jesus, thank you for coming to us. Thank you for the new life you have placed deep within our hearts. Thank you for the laws of that life. We want to follow you and be led by the Holy Spirit. Thank you for our traditions, but may they never come in the way of our obedience to you. We decide now to be led by you rather than the laws of our traditions. Thank you for setting us free to go with you. We decide now to follow you. Amen.

CHAPTER 8

FOOLISH GALATIANS

We have seen that we are not saved *by* works but *for* works by the work of Jesus and our faith in what He has accomplished for us. Now that we have been saved by Him for works that He appoints us to, it is easy in our eagerness to be involved in His work and service to get ourselves involved in works that He has not appointed us to or to think that we are establishing our relationship with God through these works or even maintaining our relationship with God through these activities.

Our relationship with God is not attained to by religious activity nor is it maintained by religious activity, but by faith. At first this statement may seem almost shocking to some. To some, indeed, it will be shocking just as the parable that Jesus told about the Pharisee who put his trust in his religious activity and the publican whose only hope was the mercy of God, was shocking to the people of His day.

In the letter to the Galatians, the apostle Paul wrote to a beautiful group of Christians who had experienced great blessing in the Lord when they believed the gospel that he proclaimed to them. This particular church had experienced many miracles and demonstrations of the Holy Spirit's presence among them. It was glorious. Then something happened.

The power of the Spirit waned, the beautiful sense of blessing and God's presence left. What went wrong? This group had enjoyed such joy and holy liberty in the presence of God and then it all seemed to dry up.

The message of the cross and the redemption that was theirs through the work of Jesus had brought them such joy and freedom. Now that joy was leaving them and their freedom was beginning to go. Apparently, some other Jewish believers in Jesus had come to the Galatians and told them that it was not enough for them to have faith in the work that Jesus did on the cross, to be filled with the Holy Spirit and to live pure and holy lives. They must also keep the Old Covenant Laws.

Now the Old Covenant had been given to man through Moses to make us aware of our need for God, but the New Covenant was given to fill that need. The Old Covenant was given to us to show us the need of a Redeemer, but the New Covenant proclaims that the Redeemer has come. Under the Old Covenant men tried to establish and maintain a relationship with God through their religious activity.

Under the New Covenant the relationship is a gift through faith which is maintained through faith. It is lived out in Christlike activity. This Christlike activity is the fruit of the relationship and not the means by which the relationship is created.

The Galatian church continued in the freedom of the gospel Paul had taught until some other teachers told them that the only way to maintain their relationship with God was through religious activity. The freedom of faith began to be replaced by the straining of religious activity. They began to try to get closer to God by returning to the law of Moses and obeying all kinds of do's and don't's.

The effect of this was to bring them from a life of faith and trust in Jesus and the grace of God to a life of trusting in themselves. Now they were still Christians. They still called Jesus Lord and professed faith in Him, but by their actions they were trusting more in themselves and their religious acts to maintain their life in the Spirit than their faith in Jesus.

Paul, in his letter to the Galatians, expresses great anger at this corruption of the gospel that was stealing the Galatians' joy. He writes: *"You are severed from Christ, you who would be justified by the law; you have fallen away from grace"* (Galatians 5:4).

This going back to do's and don't's, while it may appear as very holy and righteous activity, has the effect of severing rather than establishing a relationship with God for one who has come to believe and be blessed through the saving work of Christ.

The story of the Galatians' fall from grace through a return to 'do-it-yourselfism' is the story of much of the history of the church throughout the ages and in our own time. How often God has graciously poured out his Spirit to humble and hungry hearts, only to have those people revert to all kinds of contrived religious activity to maintain their blessing.

Much of the religious activity, church attendance, witnessing, and Bible study that goes on in the church today is a form of 'going back under the law'. It is an effort to establish or enhance a relationship with God through these activities. If church attendance, witnessing, Bible study and other religious acts are being entered into by believers to establish a relationship with God, then these activities will be counterproductive and will weaken rather that strengthen our faith. If we are using our religious activities in this way, then we are making the same error that the Galatians made and the presence of God in our lives will weaken.

On the other hand, if we use Bible study, church attendance and witnessing to express and celebrate the relationship with God that we already have, then we will experience these activities to be uplifting and encouraging and the presence of Christ in our lives will be strengthened.

How subtle the difference between these two attitudes towards religious activity and yet how great the difference.

If you have become a foolish Galatian, return to your first love and put all your trust in the grace of God and not in your conduct or knowledge. Let the presence of Christ manifest and shine forth radiantly in all you do.

Today the church needs to repent from its religion (that is its self-righteousness and effort towards self-improvement through so called Christian activity) as much as it needs to repent of its sinfulness and sins. Remember, it was not through any obvious sins that the Galatians lost their sense of blessing but through going back to precepts and ordinances to establish or maintain their relationship with God.

Jesus had forseen that many people in the church would succumb to this form of spiritual decay which resembles godliness when he warned: *"Beware of the leaven of the Pharisees which is hypocrisy. Nothing is covered up that will not be revealed or hidden that will not be known"* (Luke 12:1-2). Hypocrisy is often confused with insincerity. In fact, it is something quite different.

Many hypocritical people are really sincere in what they are doing. Hypocrisy is the attempt to act differently than what one really is. In the process of doing this, one becomes deceived into thinking that he is the person he has been pretending to be. This is hypocrisy. It is a frequent disease among those who seek to be godly. It occurs when people behave in a religious manner and thereby think that they have come close to God. The Galatians got infected with this disease, and Paul therefore warns them that godly behavior is the fruit of the Holy Spirit's presence in their lives and cannot be produced by religious striving.

There once was a very happy married couple. They were deeply in love with each other, delighted to do many things for each other, and could never get enough of each other's company. The husband would work long hours to provide well for his bride and plan many special outings where they could be together. The wife, for her part, delighted in her homemaking and the thousand details that made their house into a home. Time went by and they still loved each other just as much.

Then one day they were invited to attend a marriage seminar. They did not really feel they needed the seminar but they went along anyway to please their friends. The counselor seemed very learned and knowledgeable about his subject. He spoke about communication, assertiveness, role conflict and all manner of subjects that our happy couple had never heard about.

"If you do all that I tell you" said the counselor, who himself had had three marriages, "your marriage will improve greatly. Each day write down on a piece of paper all the faults you see in your spouse and at the end of each week show him the list. This will ensure open communication in your marriage."

The happy couple of our story took the counselor's advice. They noticed faults in each other and in themselves that they had overlooked before. They openly shared this with each other and then they began to defend themselves against these new accusations. The marriage did not break up. The couple did not believe in divorce, but they separated and the communication between them collapsed.

A few months went by. They remembered the happy times that they had had together before they went to the marriage seminar. "Let's be simple," they said. "Let's just love one another and that love will teach us once again how to be one." They cried, they hugged, they laughed and from that day on,they lived in perfect harmony together.

The Galatian Christians, like many of us, had the experience of falling in love with God through the message of the gospel and the work of the Holy Spirit, but had fallen back to legal works to create a relationship they already had and, in the process, weakened that relationship.

Today the church is returning to its first love. There is much teaching of do's and don't's and complex psychology and theology that would steal us from the joy of our simple relationship with Christ. Teachers will come by with new formulae for holiness or faith to try to make us work our way closer to God. We cannot get closer to God by any other way than the way that has been opened up by the cross of Jesus. Let us live in that happy position and from that position let us bless and go to the people of our world.

What then is the place of religious activity in the life of the church? When do we fall into the error of the 'foolish Galatians' and when are we exercising right Christian discipline?

Whenever we use anything less than, or other than, our faith in the work of Jesus on the cross as the means of establishing our relationship with God, we have reverted to something other than Jesus as our source of redemption and strayed from a pure relationship with Him. On the other hand, there is a right use of church activity and discipline in the life of every believer.

"Let us hold fast the confession of our hope without wavering, for He who promised is faithful; and let us consider how to stir up one another to love and good works, not neglecting to meet together as in the habit of some, but encouraging one another and all the more as you see the Day drawing near" (Hebrews 10:23-25).

There is a need to come together and to work together that we may grow in the knowledge and understanding of our relationship with God. We need to continually renew our minds and learn to walk in a manner that is in accord with our relationship with God.

As we live with others in the church, we learn to obey authority and submit to the rules of the groups with which we are associated. This is for right order because those in leadership have a responsibility to God and are placed in authority in the church by God to help us grow in grace and closeness to God.

As long as we are members of any Christian religious organization, we should abide by the rules and procedures of that group provided that it is never implied that our relationship with God is built on our relationship with that group. When that is taught, the group has overstepped its mark.

Let us hold fast to the liberty that Christ has given us, obeying right authority as long as we are called to remain there and its precepts do not call us to compromise our primary obedience to Jesus as our Lord. Do not let any person or group usurp the primary place of Jesus in your life. In these days the true liberty of the Christian is threatened on the one hand by an undisciplined and self-indulgent license, and on the other extreme by a rigid legalism occasionally demanded by some exercising the pastoral ministry.

Be free, be humble, be loving, and be dead to the works of the flesh and you will always maintain a life of holy excitement experiencing daily the presence and the power and the comfort of the Holy Spirit.

CHAPTER 9

THE TREE OF LIFE
PART I

LED BY THE SPIRIT

Since the life of Christ has come to us, we must learn to walk in a new pattern of obedience to Him who has now become our Head and Leader. The old obedience was an obedience to external regulations, the new obedience is to the directions of the Head, Jesus. Paul called this new obedience, *"the obedience of faith"* (Romans 1:5).

Many Christians see God's work in terms of His powerful acts of mercy and rescue of us. We tend to see Him in terms of what He has done for us, yet God has a fuller purpose in His plan for each of us. His fuller purpose in redeeming us is that we would and could live in obedience to Him just as Jesus lived, and that in so doing we would show forth His character and life.

The apostle Paul did not define his ministry in terms of proclaiming the saving work of Jesus and the mighty work of our redemption that He accomplished on the cross. Although this most assuredly was Paul's ministry, his definition was in terms of bringing all people into obedience to Him. God saves us to bring us under His rulership because we can enter into the fulness of what He has destined for us only if we are in subjection to Him.

This obedience of faith comes about as we learn to follow the inner direction of our new spiritual hearts. In the Christian walk of faith, there is never any question of following external voices. Any genuine external revelations or exhortations will serve not to direct us but to confirm what we hear the Spirit saying to us. It is therefore vitally important to each of us that we learn to be led by the Holy Spirit in all that we do.

"For all who are led by the spirit of God are sons of God" (Romans 8:14). There is no more important lesson for the Spirit-filled believer than to learn how to be led by the Spirit for this is the life we have been called to and equipped for in Christ.

In the book of Genesis, the scriptures tell us how man's fall from fellowship with God came about. Adam and Eve had been placed in a beautiful garden to live. Their every need was supplied there, and they were able to ask God about anything they needed to know. However, they did not have the kind of union that we can now enjoy in the kingdom of God.

In the kingdom of God, in the realm of the new creation, we know God through His Spirit who dwells within us. In the first creation, Adam and Eve spoke to God outside of themselves. In the new creation, we have been lifted up into such union with God that as long as we abide in that union, we are extensions of the life of God in human form.

Everything was beautiful and peaceful for Adam and Eve in their garden paradise. *"And the Lord God planted a garden in Eden in the east; and there He put the man whom He had formed. And out of the ground the*

Lord God made to grow every tree that is pleasant to the sight and good for food, the tree of life also in the midst of the garden and the tree of the knowledge of good and evil. And the Lord God commanded the man, saying: 'You may freely eat of every tree of the garden; but of the tree of the knowledge of good and evil you shall not eat, for in the day that you eat of it you shall die'" (Genesis 2:8-10,16-17).

Some time after this, the tempter, in the form of a serpent, said to the woman, *"You wiall not die. For God knows that when you eat of it your eyes will be opened, and you will be like God, knowing good and evil"* (Genesis 3:4-5).

We are all familiar with the outcome. Their eyes were opened, and they fell from their happy position of fellowship with God. Taking a closer look at what happened, we can see that their fall was caused by a desire *to be like God knowing good and evil.* It was not eating of any ordinary fruit tree that brought about their fall. It was a decision they made to have their lives guided by their own knowledge and understanding rather than the voice of God.

This has been the primary sin of man ever since Eden. We prefer to be guided by our own clouded minds rather than by the clear voice of God.

Man has never had a desire to do evil as such. We can assume that Adam and Eve had no direct motive towards evil. Even in their desire to know good and evil for themselves apart from the guidance of God, their intention was to choose good and avoid evil. Since then man has guided his life by his own understanding rather that the voice of God.

The mind is, of course, one of the greatest gifts that God has given us. Most people would see nothing wrong in the attempt to guide one's life by understanding and reason. To this day this is the predominant way by which men guide their lives. As wonderful as the gift of intellect is, man was destined from the beginning to be guided by God through His Spirit.

Man is a spirit who has a mind, and a body in which he lives. Man's spirit was made for fellowship and communication with God, and through this communication his life was to be guided. When we share this truth, people are surprised. They think that in saying that we were destined to be guided by something higher than our minds that we are being anti-intellectual.

This, of course, is not true. We believe that the mind has a most important part to play in our lives, but not as the highest authority. If we were to assert that though our eyes are a great and wonderful gift, they are not to be the source of our decisions and choices, no one would accuse us of being against the use of our eyes. In a similar way when we assert, in accordance with the scriptures, that man was destined to be guided by something (someone) higher than his own mind, we are not, of course, against the right use of the mind but against any attempt by the mind to take the place of God.

Sometime ago, we became quite disturbed over the lack of joy, as well as the emotional and mental heaviness we observe in many Christians. As we pondered these things, the Holy Spirit brought to our attention the events of the fall of Adam and Eve from the garden of Eden. We saw that new creation men and women are often making the same mistake as first creation man and woman. They, too, are frequently eating from the tree of the knowledge of good and evil rather than abiding at the tree of life to which they now have access.

When we eat of the tree of the knowledge of good and

evil, we are guiding our lives and judging our situations by our reasoning minds instead of by the Spirit and Word of God. Whenever we put our minds above God's revelation and voice, we are eating of the tree of knowledge of good and evil. When Adam and Eve did this, they lost their fellowship with God and their position in the garden of Eden.

Sometimes, perhaps, when we consider the sin of Adam and Eve, we may begin to think that it is really unfair that we should be the victims of their sin and that should we ever be in a similar situation we would never do what they did. The fact of the matter, however, is that we continually make the same mistakes they made whenever we choose to be led by the knowledge of good and evil (fleshly decisions) rather than by the Spirit and the Word of God.

Often we believe that if we can succeed in doing good and avoiding evil that we will automatically be pleasing God. The world is filled with 'good' people and 'nice' people who are dedicated to doing good and avoiding evil but who are yet not in the kingdom of God.

The kingdom of God is not only the realm where we live under the care of God, it is also the realm where we live under His authority. We can be very busy doing 'good' things and 'important' things and miss the best thing. If we are living at the level of the tree of the knowledge of good and evil, we shall be satisfied with doing good things. However, in so doing we can completely miss God.

Our call is not a call to do good and avoid evil, but a call *"to hear the Word of God and keep it"*, (Luke 11:28) and to be led by the Spirit of God. *"For all who are led by the Spirit of God"* (Romans 8:14).

Of all the thousand and one good things we could be

doing, how can we select the ones we are really called to do? The only way we can make the right choices is through being led and guided by the Spirit of God into those works and activities that God Himself has appointed to us. *"For we are his workmanship, created in Christ Jesus for good works, which God prepared beforehand, that we should walk in them"* (Ephesians 2:10).

In the kingdom of God we let God do the choosing. He will never choose anything evil for us to do, of course, but there are many good things that He will not assign to us.

Can you imagine a soldier joining an army and then engaging himself in every aspect of the work there? If the soldier were to involve himself in another man's assignment, he could cause much confusion for himself and others. The sentryman, for example, must remain at his post when all is calm and quiet even if the cook could use more help in the kitchen.

To be involved in good activity is not enough. We must also know that we are doing that which we have been assigned by God. No member of the body acts independently of the head. If any member were to act independently, the result would by chaotic. Imagine what would happen if our eyes were to decide to take a rest when we are driving home at night, or our legs decided to take a walk when we are trying to talk to a friend.

Yet we see much of this erratic and uncoordinated behavior in the body of Christ because the various parts of the body choose to make their own decisions so often rather than being guided by the Head.

God is calling us to the the kingdom of God, to the place where we can be led directly by Him rather than by the choices of our independent thinking. He has a higher purpose for our actions than that which the mind can conceive. The surrendered Christian will use his mind to choose those directives revealed by the Spirit and the Word, and to test each one with the scriptures to be sure that he is really hearing the Word of God.

In all of this, the mind, though it freely subordinates itself to the Word of God and the Lordship of Christ, does not remain passive or blank. The mind investigates what is written in the scriptures and distinguishes between the voice of God and that of the clamoring pressures of the world. The Christian also renews his mind through the engrafted Word and tests all things with the scriptures and the Holy Spirit.

Finally the Christian uses his mind to choose to obey and yield to God's choices and directives. The mind has indeed a most important part to play in every Christian's life. We do not suppress the mind, but subordinate it to the leadership of Christ.

The Christian functions through a subordinate mind. This is a mind that is freely and deliberately subordinate to the Lordship of Christ as revealed through the Spirit in harmony with the scriptures. This does NOT mean that the Christian should blank out his mind and receive every thought and suggestion that comes into his mind as if it were the voice of God.

Some believers fall into a passive state of mind and do not keep it active in its right place. Such Christians act as if they did not have a mind and are, therefore, very open to deception. In this state he may fall into the trap of surrendering his decision making to some other person, as it happens in some cults, or even to demon spirits. Though we are to be led by the Spirit and not by our minds, we are to engage our minds in the search of what is the mind of God in any particular matter. We do this by searching the scriptures, listening to the witness of the

Spirit in our hearts, praying for clearer guidance from the Lord, listening to the advice of pastors and mature friends in the Lord, releasing our own likes and preferences, renewing our consecration, and finally choosing God's choice.

To be led by the Spirit is not something 'spooky' or super mystical. For the man in Christ, it is naturally supernatural and supernaturally natural because God has written His laws 'deep within our hearts' at the time of our new birth. Since His Spirit has come to abide in us, the voice of God is nearer to us than we are to ourselves.

When we were born from above our spirits became one spirit with the Spirit of Christ, for *"he who is united to the Lord becomes one spirit with him"* (I Corinthians 6:17). Just as our body 'speaks' to us when it needs rest or food, so too our spirits when united to the Spirit of the Lord, speak to us when the Lord wants to direct us in anything. When we are in the will of God, or when the Lord wants us to continue on with what we are doing, He gives us deep peace in our hearts. *"Let the peace of Christ rule in your hearts to which indeed you were called in the one body"* (Colossians 3:15).

So God communicates to us who have received the new birth through our spirits. This speaking is not generally in an audible voice or prophecies but in the gentle nudging of His Spirit within us. God can, of course and sometimes does, speak in an audible voice or through a prophecy, but even these forms of communication will serve only to confirm the inner nudging of the Spirit within our hearts and will never be a substitute for it.

An Illustration

Once there was a handsome young salmon who had

been spawned in a mountain stream in Ireland. How he enjoyed his mountain streams and the deep pools and splashing waterfalls. As time went by, however, he began to feel somewhat uneasy. The stirrings of adventure began to move deep within him and the desire to travel the vast salt ocean began to awaken within him. Swimming downstream with the rapid current of the river he began his long, long journey; a journey that would take him across the vast waters of the Atlantic even to the far off exotic islands of the Caribbean.

More time went by, and the desire to return home now began to stir within him. He began to swim north by northeast. He did not really know exactly which direction he was moving in, he just knew he was headed towards the tinkling streams of his Irish hills. And so he returned.

When he returned, the stories of his travels in distant lands were circulated among the fish that swam and lived in the mountain lakes and streams. Among them was an ambitious young perch. He heard of the exploits of the salmon and he decided to emulate them. He prepared for his journey meticulously, by much study of oceanography and navigation. Finally he too set out on his journey of adventure. Filled with confidence, and sure of his calculations and preparations, he began to swim as no perch had ever swam. Soon he was unmistakably lost and hopelessly confused. The perch knew more about navigation than any salmon and yet he was lost. He had been guided by his learned knowledge while the salmon had been guided by the inner law of his being.

When we are born again, the inner life of God's Spirit is implanted deep within us and as we obey this new inner law, the law of the spirit of life in Christ Jesus, we must perfectly fulfill God's plan for us. However, the programming of our intellect or the pull of our emotion can tend to pull us away from this law, so we must continue to remain attuned to this new inner law which is far more intelligent than our highest reason or the lust of our emotions.

As we live at the tree of life we return to this law of God and move in obedience to the emotions or the opinion of our intellect. God has offered us a tremendous gift in offering to us the gift of his own Spirit to dwell within us to guide us into all truth and to lead us down the road of our destiny. To be led by the Spirit we will put our minds in second place and surrender our beings to the highest guidance principle of all - God Himself who made us to be guided and directed by Himself and not by our own intellect. By placing His law within us and restoring us to open fellowship with Himself, He has brought us back to the tree of life, and redeemed us from the tree of the knowledge of good and evil which has been the source of our confusion and striving.

CHAPTER 10

THE TREE OF LIFE
PART II

Redeemed from Good and Evil

Let us now take another look at these two spiritual trees that are mentioned in the book of Genesis, the tree of life and the tree of the knowledge of good and evil. We have already seen that God has made us to be guided and directed by His Spirit, and not by our reasoning minds (the tree of the knowledge of good and evil). Not only are our lives not to be directed by our minds alone, but they are not to be analyzed, measured, or judged in terms of 'good and evil' either.

Many honest people live their lives with many regrets about the past. They blame themselves for mistakes they have made or perhaps they feel that their lives have been ruined or thwarted by various injustices or 'bad breaks'. We can, of course, analyze all the events that have gone into our lives in terms of good and evil. We can analyze our position and condition today in terms of good and evil. To do so, however, is not helpful.

If we were to analyze our past history in terms of good and evil, we might perhaps assess it as follows: 'I

had a reasonably good childhood but my parents neg-
lected certain matters in their care of me, as a result of
which......' or 'My childhood was partly good and partly
bad. I am happy about the good parts, but I regret the bad
parts, for there is nothing I can do now to undo the damage. My education was also partly good and partly bad. I
am happy that I had some wonderful teachers, but others
were not so good and did much damage to my self-confidence, etc. etc.'

Many people tend to analyze their life experiences in
these terms. They see their lives as a mixture of good and
bad, of ups and downs. Each day is seen as partly good
and partly evil, and so it is reckoned as partly successful
and happy and partly not. Since this is the way they consider life to be, they resign themselves to being partly
happy and partly unhappy, partly frustrated. Even the
happiest of men have had some evil touch their lives, or
make some irreversible mistakes at some point, and so
even they consider themselves to be partly victims of the
evil that is in the world.

This kind of analysis of our lives in terms of good and
evil may be quite accurate and true, but it is an analysis
that is not helpful and which produces hopelessness and
regret. God is calling us away from the tree of the knowledge of good and evil. He is making it possible for us to
come away from it. He is calling us away from our regrets
and 'if only's' to the tree of life which is the realm of faith
and of this working redemption of all things in our lives.

If we choose to live in the realm of the tree of the
knowledge of good and evil, there are four possible explanations we can give to explain every difficult circumstance in our lives.

(1) We can blame them on ourselves.

(2) We can blame them on someone else (parents, teachers, social systems, political leaders, church leaders, spouse, employers, enemies, etc.).

(3) We can blame them on the devil.

(4) We can attribute them to God.

Usually, if we attempt this kind of analysis of our problems, we will come up with an explanation that is a combination of some or all of these. Such explanations may be accurate, but they have little power to remedy the situation.

If we come to the tree of life on the other hand, we come to the realm where we release ourselves into the realm of God's mighty working and redeeming ability and away from our vain analyses and futile regrets. Instead of apportioning blame and 'licking our wounds', we yield all situations into the hands of God who makes *"all things work together for good for those who love him"* (Romans 8:28). This is the amazing condition and privilege of those who live in the kingdom of God. Here in this realm ALL things, yes, ALL things, the evil as well as the good are working together for our good as we abide in Him and continue to release all to Him.

Instead of living on the two-way street of good and evil, we who believe can now live in a wonderful dimension where we are on a one-way street of blessing in which everything is a blessing to us. We can truthfully say that from now on, for the rest of our lives and for all eternity that we shall never meet a person or a situation that is not going to be a blessing to us. Everything that will happen to us and every person we shall ever meet is going to be a blessing to us as long as we remain under the Lordship of Christ our Redeemer, and continue to surrender all things to God for Him to bless, use and redeem.

We are not, of course, saying that we can never be touched by evil again or that we have discovered some magic vaccine that immunizes us from evil. What we are saying is that we can never encounter a situation which God won't turn into a blessing for us if we abide at the tree of life.

Jesus never promised that life with Him would be immune from evil. *"Sufficient for the day is the evil thereof"*, He said (Matthew 6:34). He also said that we would have tribulation in this world, but that tribulation would not destroy us and would work for our good (John 16:33).

Our lives may be touched by the evil that is still in the world, but as we remain in union with Him, that evil will not destroy our lives but will actually be made to work for our good. *"I have said this to you that in me you may have peace. In the world you have tribulation; but be of good cheer, I have overcome the world"* (John 16:33).

Whenever we turn our evil situations over to God for Him to use, He works in it for our good. It is not what happens to us so much as how we react to what happens to us that makes it a blessing. This is not a mere positive thinking technique, but the true response of one who is living in faith in God's ability to turn all good and evil things into blessings for us.

In the church we talk much about Jesus as our Savior and about Jesus as our Lord. We need also to allow Him to be continually our Redeemer. He is the one who can take all that has gone into our lives, and all that is now going on in our lives, under His control and use it all to advance His purpose in our lives, and so to bless us if we let Him. He takes all of the evil that has touched our lives, whether it was caused by ourselves or by others, and, as we release it to Him, makes it better that all these things happened than if they never happened.

In today's society there is much emphasis placed on discoveries made in the realm of psychology. To understand things from a psychological point of view can be of help to some. It is often a help and a crutch for the natural (Adamian) man. However for the born from above, new creation believer, psychology can become a temptation to 'munch' from the tree of the knowledge of good and evil. The harmful effects of lacks or deprivations and wounding experiences in our lives are considered by psychologists to be minuses to us. The psychologist may help us to recognize, admit and confront these 'lacks' in us and thereby learn to cope with them. However, the more we analyze in this realm, the more evident our 'minuses' become.

While the psychologist may help us to cope with and compensate for the hurts of our lives, no modern psychological technique can give us the deep inner healing of all wounds to our psyche that we can receive through the redemptive work of Jesus as we abide at the tree of life. When we come away from the realm of analysis, introspection and blame apportionment that is the mark of those who live at the tree of the knowledge of good and evil and come to Jesus, all our 'minuses' (psychological and otherwise) can be turned into pluses. As we release all to His touch, receive His forgiveness and, in turn, forgive others, and receive the new creation life He gives, we are released from the hurts of the past and their effects on our lives, and we can truly experience that God makes all things *work together for good* even deprived childhoods and hurtful experiences, as we release all to the redemptive touch of Christ.

Most of us are familiar with the legend of King Midas. He was granted the fulfillment of his wish that everything he touched would turn to gold. Whatever he touched turned to gold. If he were to touch a bushel of silver, it would turn to a bushel of gold; if he were to touch a bushel of trash it too would turn to gold. No matter what came in contact with his fingers, valuable or worthless, it would turn to gold.

The legend of King Midas is, of course, only a story, a piece of fiction. The story of King Jesus our Redeemer king, is, far from being a mere story, the central fact of history. As we give Him the scars of our lives, He turns them into the gold of blessing. Give Him our happiness, and He will make it a twice blessed happiness. Give Him our pains and sorrows, and disappointments, and He will turn them into assets, *For my strength is made perfect in weakness"* (II Corinthians 12:9). As our Redeemer, He not only redeems us from our sins, but He touches all the evil, and injustices and mistakes of our lives and makes them work for our good.

It is critically important that we come away from the tree of the knowledge of good and evil. As we remain at this tree our lives remain filled with bitterness and regret. Surely the fruit of this tree is more bitter than the most bitter herb. As we eat from it, it fills us with regrets and 'if only's'. ('If only I had studied harder at school', 'If only my parents had had more income', 'If only I had made a different career choice', 'If only I had not been treated so unfairly', 'If only I had invested my money differently', 'If only.....') At the tree of life, we come away from all our 'if only's' to Jesus with His redemptive touch, and we see Him take all that has ever gone into our lives, forgive us of our personal liability, and make it all work for good.

Let us not look at the cross of Jesus, and imply by our regrets that He did not do enough. *"It is finished"* (John 19:30). He is more than a conqueror over all the good and evil in our lives.

"Who shall separate us from the love of Christ? Shall tribulation, or distress, or persecution, or famine, or nakedness, or peril, or sword? As it is written, 'For thy sake we are being killed all the day long; we are regarded as sheep to be slaughtered.' No, in all these things we are more than conquerors through Him who loved us. For I am sure that neither death, nor life, nor angels, nor principalities, nor things present, nor things to come, nor powers, nor height, nor depth, nor anything else in all creation, will be able to separate us from the love of God in Christ Jesus our Lord" (Romans 8:35-39).

It is only in the dimension of the tree of life that we can truly forgive and live the forgiving life. Often we try to forgive but our minds remain filled with regret that this unwanted event took place.

We say, "I forgive", but inside we are thinking: "I want to forgive, but that person has done me much harm which can never be undone." However, when we KNOW that God takes the injustices, the heartbreaks and the disappointments of life into His mighty hands to make it better that they happened than if they had never happened, then we KNOW that the painful experience can become a blessing in our lives. In this context it is easy to forgive as we release all to Him.

A great example of this truth is found in the Old Testament in the life of Joseph. After Joseph received the coat of many colors from his father, you will recall how his brothers became violently jealous. They threw him in a pit and sold him to some wandering merchants who took him off to Egypt. You recall also the injustices that befell him there and how he was wrongfully accused and thrown into jail. Yet God used all these apparent misfortunes, promoted Joseph to a very high place of influence and finally used him to rescue his entire family.

Joseph must have wondered why all these things were happening to him as he went through these testing experiences. Perhaps he thought that there was some deep flaw in his personality or that he had done something to remove himself from the blessing of God. Perhaps the devil had destroyed the promise of his early years or that he was the victim of a bad family or bad court and prison system.

If Joseph were given to eating of the tree of the knowledge of good and evil, there is no doubt that his mind would have wandered down all these negative labyrinths. However, Joseph did not rebel against all these inexplicable misfortunes that seemed to continually befall him. He did not eat of the tree of the knowledge of good and evil but entrusted his cause to God.

In the end he was able to say to his brothers, *"Fear not, for am I in the place of God— As for you, you meant evil against me; but God meant it for good, to bring it about that many people should be kept alive as they are today"* (Genesis 50:19-20). Joseph knew that what man and the devil and the circumstance of life had been directing towards evil, God had been shaping to work for good in the life of this called man who trusted Him so steadfastly.

The greatest example of this truth, however, is Jesus Himself especially in the events of His crucifixion and resurrection. Before He finally submitted to this dreadful fate, Jesus went to His Father to inquire once more if there was any way in which He could avoid it.

"Father, if thou art willing, remove this cup from

me; nevertheless not my will but thine be done" (Luke 22:42). Later before Pilate, He said: *"You would have no power over me unless it had been given you from above..,"* (John 19:11) thus showing that He was receiving it from His Father above and not from secondary causes.

From the point of view of the knowledge of good and evil, we would say that the death of Jesus was the most evil thing. We would say that Jesus was the victim of the disloyalty of His followers, the betrayal of Judas, and the corrupt state of the religious and political establishment. If ever the devil had caused anything, this surely was his work.

Jesus, however, did not live in the realm of the tree of the knowledge of good and evil, but received all things through His Father's hands releasing everything to Him. We know that God took all these evil events and turned them around to work our redemption. What the devil intended as evil, God used for the good of all of us. Even from the standpoint of Jesus' personal life, God used those who were the instruments of His death to press Him on to resurrection. *"Jesus for the joy that was set before Him endured the cross, despising the shame, and is seated at the right hand of the throne of God"* (Hebrews 12:2).

Abide in Him, and see yourself no longer in the up and down life of those who live in the realm of the tree of the knowledge of good and evil. As a believer, you are now in the kingdom of God. See yourself as being under the care of God and under the Lordship and redemptive ability of Jesus Christ where all things are working together for your good.

As we come away from the double vision of the tree of the knowledge of good and evil, we can come into the blessed single vision that Jesus spoke about. *"The eye is the lamp of the body. So if your eye is single, your body is full of light"*(Matthew 6:22).

God wants us to see all things in the light of His Lordship and Redemption, and to be able to say with the apostle Paul: *"Who shall separate us from the love of Christ? Shall tribulation, or distress, or persecution, or famine, or nakedness, or peril, or sword? As it is written, For thy sake we are being killed all the day long; we are regarded as sheep to be slaughtered. No in all these things we are more than conquerors through him who loved us. For I am sure that neither death, not life, nor angels, not principalities, nor things present, nor things to come, nor powers, nor height, nor depth, nor anything else in all creation, will be able to separate us from the love of God in Christ Jesus our Lord"* (Romans 8:35-39).

A prayer

Lord, we release to you all that has gone into our lives, the good and the evil, the disappointments and the triumphs, every injustice that anyone has done agasinst us, any mistaken decision we may have taken, and we receive your forgiveness and forgive ourselves and any who may have harmed us. Now Lord we trust you to redeem all the liabilities of our lives completely, and make them work together for our good. We see ourselves no longer as victims of our own mistakes and others but under your Lordship where even the worst mistakes are being made over by you to advance your purposes in our lives.

Amen. Hallelujah.

PART III

THE GLORY

CHAPTER 11

THE CALL TO BE OVERCOMERS

The Lord is preparing a victorious overcoming church on the earth today. These will be people who are filled with and anointed with God's Holy Spirit, dead to self, victorious over sin, filled with love and led by the Holy Spirit.

In the early part of the book of Revelation, the apostle John describes a vision he had when he was in exile on the island of Patmos. No doubt in the long days of his exile, he must have thought back on the events of his life. A generation had passed since the resurrection of Jesus and the birth of the church. Where was it all going and when would Jesus return to be united with His spiritual bride to set up His visible kingdom on earth? Jesus had not yet returned. Much of the fervor and enthusiasm of the early years of the church had evaporated. In this context, Jesus appeared to John in a vision and showed him in symbolic form the unfolding of God's plan on the earth for John's own day as well as for far off generations.

In this vision, Jesus also brought messages for the churches (Revelation, Chapter 2 and 3). He was aware of the various weaknesses of the churches. He promised that if anyone from any of the churches would be willing to overcome as He had overcome, that person would become a ruler with Him in the coming ages.

He would use those who would follow Him faithfully. He was preparing overcomers everywhere through whom He could get His work done.

This pattern of using a few faithful people to spearhead His work is a familiar pattern of God's working throughout the scriptures (such as Gideon's army). There is no need for the number of overcomers to be a small number (as was Gideon's army), however, because the call to be an overcomer is open to all believers and is, in fact, the highest call of all.

The apostle Paul considered this call to be the high call of his life and esteemed it higher even than his call to be a preacher and an apostle. The ministry of the overcomer will last throughout the ages for he will be a ruler and reigner with Jesus.

In fact the purpose of the ministry of those in the offices of ministry today is to produce overcomers, mature saints walking on this earth in the pattern of Jesus (Ephesians 4:12-13). *"Not that I have already obtained this,"* the apostle Paul writes, *"or am already perfect; but I press on to make it my own, because Christ Jesus has made me his own. Brethren, I do not consider that I have made it my own; but one thing I do, forgetting what lies behind and straining forward to what lies ahead, I press on toward the goal for the prize of the upward call of God in Christ Jesus. Let those of us who are mature be thus minded"* (Philippians 3:12-15).

The prize of the high call is his goal, which is *"that I may know Him and the power of His resurrection, and may share his sufferings, becoming like him in his death, that if possible I may attain the resurrection from the dead"* (Philippians 3:11).

According to Jesus' words to John in the book of Revelation, the overcomers can be found in every kind of denomination. They do not constitute a new "group" with a higher or superior revelation, but they are the maturing church found in almost every denomination.

Today, as in the latter years of the apostle John (Revelations, Chapter 2 and 3), some churches are cold, lukewarm, hard or in partial error and yet even in these churches one can find some who are faithfully and wholeheartedly living out their love union with God.

Jesus promises the overcomers special blessings. The overcomers will:

(1) *"eat of the tree of life"* (Rev. 2:7)

(2) *"not be hurt by the second death"* (Rev. 2:11)

(3) *"be given some of the hidden manna and a new name written on a white stone"* (Rev. 2:17)

(4) *"be given power over the nations and shall rule them with a rod of iron"* (Rev. 2:26)

(5) *"be clad in white garments"* and their names *"will not be blotted out from the book of life."* (Rev. 3:5)

(6) *"be made a pillar in the temple"* (Rev.3:12)

(7) *"sit with Me (Jesus) on My throne as I conquered and sat with the Father on His throne"* (Rev. 3:21)

It is clear from these scriptures that the overcomers will rule and reign with Jesus in His coming kingdom. They overcome as Jesus Himself overcame. *"They overcame him by the blood of the Lamb, and the word of their testimony; and they loved not their lives unto the death."* (Revelation 12:11 KJV)

Like Jesus, they are determined to live out their call to walk on this earth as sons of God in radical obedience to the leading of the Holy Spirit and in the example of Jesus and in fidelity to His teachings. For the overcomer, Jesus is more than Savior, Lord and Baptizer. He is also the pattern on which they model their lives.

John writes: *"As he is so are we in this world"* (1 John 4:17). If we understand what this means, we will see that Jesus is calling us to live on the earth in the same manner that He Himself did. Though we do not live in the same culture in which He lived or have the same mission that He had, we are to be *in the world as He is.*

We are in the world as He is in the world because we are connected to the resources of heaven and the presence of God as Jesus was. We have become partakers in the divine nature that Jesus has. Since we have been born from above, we are not of this world and have the same relationship with it that Jesus had. We are being sent into it in the same way that Jesus has been sent into it.

"As the Father has sent me, even so I send you" (John 20:21). We go into the world in the same way that Jesus went into it, as ones whose home and supply is from heaven. Jesus is the first to have a relationship with the world. He is our model and His life is the pattern for our new lives. We now live in the world with the same relationship with the Father, the world and the devil which Jesus has.

In our study of the temptations of Jesus, we see that Jesus overcame the world, the flesh, and the devil simply by abiding in union with His Father and obeying Him. Even though that obedience cost him disgrace, misunderstanding, humiliation and death, He did not swerve from the path. Thus, He became the first overcomer and the model for all overcomers from then on.

The overcomers who will follow after Jesus will also overcome the temptations of the world, the flesh and the devil as Jesus did. This victory is achieved not by fighting these forces, but by giving them no ground in our lives. Through total reliance on the grace of God and the person of Jesus we can live in victory over them. The overcomers are not deterred from their path within the footsteps of Jesus by the noises and pressures of the world. They are not directed by popular wisdom or by the dictates of money or career, but are directed by the Holy Spirit even when that obedience is costly.

Many are called to be overcomers, but few choose it. Jesus said: *"If any man would come after me, let him deny himself and take up his cross and follow me. For whoever would save his life will lose it; and whoever loses his life for my sake will find it"* (Matthew 16:24). This is the call to radical discipleship which Jesus extends to all who are willing to follow Him, not just as admirers but with the same kind of obedience to the Father that He Himself lived in.

Though the path of the overcomer-disciple may seem like a hard and difficult way to some, it is the happiest, most carefree, fulfilling way in which any man could live. It is a narrow way, but it is also a liberated way and a glorious way. Those who choose it will know, not only the future rewards of their obedience, but a closeness to God that can be enjoyed in no other way. *"Take my yoke upon you,"* says Jesus, *"for my yoke is easy and my burden is light"* (Matthew 11:29-30).

Not all Christians are called to one of the public ministries of the church, but all are called to the highest call of all, the call to be an overcoming disciple.

Many within the church who do not have any public ministry, live lives of close union with Christ and are truly overcomers, true and pure disciples of Jesus. These people, though their lives may be hidden now and though they may be obscure and ignored, will be among those who will reign and rule with Jesus at His coming.

Of course, some of the prominent people in the church are also living overcoming lives. If so, they, too, will be in the company of those who will be closest to Jesus throughout the ages. *"But, many that are first will be last, and the last first"* (Matthew 19:30). Many of the hidden people in God's family will emerge as Jesus' co-reigners in that day when He comes to claim His kingdom.

Our greatest aim should be to live closer and closer to God through Jesus and to really seek to know Him and to be like Him. We sometimes put too much emphasis on the work of the church and not enough on its greatest mission which is to simply love God and love our brother also. Those who have really loved God in this way and have expressed that genuine love to Him and to others in various forms of service will form God's overcoming army.

Those who really want to reproduce the character of Jesus and be like Him will put obedience to God and humble service to their fellowman above every other value. Never will the work they do for God be allowed to become an end in itself or a means to social and religious power. All work will stem from a real deep knowledge of God and will be done from a motive of love and obedience to God. It is this glowing relationship with God through Jesus in the Holy Spirit that is the mark of a real disciple. The spiritual strength that we can derive from such a relationship will empower us to be victorious overcoming believers.

CHAPTER 12

THE TEMPTATIONS
OF THE CHRISTIAN

After Jesus was anointed with the Holy Spirit, He was led by the Spirit into the desert to be tempted by the devil. For forty days He encountered the devil through various temptations. These forty days were days of decision for Jesus. Here we see His deep commitment to be led only by God's Spirit in all that He was to do even if that led to a contradiction of His own human desires.

Those temptations which Jesus encountered are temptations which everyone who is filled with God's Spirit will encounter. Every Christian who is filled with and anointed with the Holy Spirit must be willing to encounter these temptations and overcome them if he wishes to be led by the Holy Spirit in a life that is effective for God.

It is sometimes implied by some of today's religious teaching that once a person is born from above and baptized with the Holy Spirit that his battles are over. The opposite was true in the life of Jesus and will also be the case in our lives if we are really sincere in our desire to be of service to God and be truly directed by His Spirit.

Let us first look at Jesus' temptations and see them not just as something that was part of His own personal history, but as a pattern for the kind of temptations that will be faced by every sincere disciple of His. *"And Jesus, full of the Holy Spirit, returned from the Jordan and was led by the Spirit for forty days in the wilderness, tempted by the devil. And he ate nothing in those days; and when they were ended, He was hungry. The devil said to Him, 'If you are the Son of God, command this stone to become bread.'*

"And Jesus answered him, 'It is written, Man shall not live by bread alone.' And the devil took him up, and showed him all the kingdoms of the world in a moment of time, and said to him, 'To you I will give all this authority and their glory; for it has been delivered to me, and I give it to whom I will. If you, then, will worship me, it shall all be yours.'

"And Jesus answered him, 'It is written, You shall worship the Lord your God, and Him only shall you serve.' And he took him to Jerusalem, and set him on the pinnacle of the temple, and said to him, 'If you are the Son of God, throw yourself down from here; for it is written, He will give his angels charge of you to guard you, and On their hands they will bear you up, lest you strike your foot against a stone.'"

"And Jesus answered him, 'It is said You shall not tempt the Lord your God.' And when the devil had ended every temptation, he departed from him until an opportune time. And Jesus returned in the power of the Spirit into Galilee" (Luke 4:1-14).

In this passage we read of three major temptations with which the devil tempted Jesus and tempts us also. The first temptation where the devil tempted Jesus to turn stones into bread can be seen as an attempt to get Jesus to concentrate on the pursuit of material prosperity before obedience to the promptings of His heavenly Father and the Word of God.

The second temptation in which Jesus is offered all the kingdoms of the earth is an attempt to draw Jesus into the pursuit of social and political power before obedience. The third temptation in which Jesus is shown the glories of Jerusalem from the pinnacle of the temple can be seen as an attempt to draw Jesus into seeking power and influence in the church before obedience.

The most subtle thing about these temptations is that each of the things with which the devil tempted Jesus were things which His Father would give to Him anyway in due time. It was definitely God's will for Jesus to have all the bread He needed. It was definitely God's will for Jesus to be at the pinnacle of the temple. He is now the head of the church. It was also God's will for Jesus to be over all the kingdoms of the earth. These are already His legal dominion and will soon be seen to be His.

Jesus, then, was tempted by the devil with things that it was the Father's good pleasure to give to Him anyway. What he was being tempted with was to pursue, or to try to attain these things through service of the devil rather than simply pursuing the will of His Father.

His temptation was, and ours is, to pursue the things which God wants to give us in due season rather than pursue the will of God. Jesus was not to pursue these things; He was to inherit them. He said: *"The meek shall inherit the earth,"* (Matthew 5:5) and He Himself asked us to learn meekness from Him. He has set us a pattern and an example of meekness and obedience. *"Take my yoke upon you and learn from me; for I am gentle and lowly in heart and you will find rest for your souls"* (Matthew 11:29).

It was not sufficient for Jesus just to know, nor is it sufficient for us just to know, that a particular thing or position is God's will for us. We must also know HOW God wants us to inherit that thing or position, and WHEN He wants us to inherit it. When many people discover that it is God's will for them to have something, they assume that they therefore have the right to pursue that thing. In so doing they can be unwittingly succumbing to the subtle temptations of the enemy. It is not enough for us to know God's ends for us, we must also know God's means.

In His temptation period, Jesus decided not to pursue anything but to obey and please His Father. He knew that as He did this, His Father would bring Him into His inheritance. He decided to pursue obedience to His Father and not the things His Father would give Him. Our temptation is to pursue that which the Father wants to give us, rather than obedience to Him. Those who seek to please God will inherit great things from Him; but for those who put those things above obedience to God, there will be great sorrow.

B   Jesus summed up the lessons of His temptation when He said: *"The Gentiles seek all these things; and your heavenly Father knows that you need them all. But seek first his kingdom and his righteousness, and all these things shall be yours as well"* (Matthew 6:32-33).

Many today are quite sure that they are not succumbing to the temptations of the devil when in fact they are. They have Jesus as their Savior. They have received reconciliation with God through the cross and they have been filled and baptized with the Holy Spirit. They would not dream of making any sort of deal with the devil and would never deny the Lord. Yet they unwittingly yield to the devil's temptations.

They follow the leading of the devil rather than the voice of God. How can this be? How can the devil influence the behavior of born again, Spirit baptized Christians?

He can do so by using the same methods he tried unsuccessfully on Jesus. He spoke to Jesus through His lustful, self-serving desires, but Jesus did not respond. The devil speaks to us in the same way through our lustful, self-serving desires. If we are not watchful we may think: "I am a believer in God. I am redeemed by the blood of Jesus. All things are lawful for me and I have scripture to back up my desire to go this way."

Thus, the unsuspecting Christian can pursue the course of action suggested by his own lustful desires and unwittingly fall into the devil's trap and veer off the course of obedience to the heavenly Father.

James tells us that when we are tempted by the devil, we are tempted by him through our lustful desires. *"Let no one say when he is tempted, 'I am tempted by God'; for God cannot be tempted with evil and He Himself tempts no one; but each person is tempted when he is lured and enticed by his own desire"* (James 1:13-14). From this passage, we can see that when Satan tempts us, he does so through our carnal desires.

When Peter urged Jesus to avoid the cross, Jesus recognized that the same temptation He had faced in the desert was being voiced again. This time it was being voiced through the sentimental concern of His friend, Peter. Jesus answered: *"Get behind me Satan! For you are not on the side of God but of men"* (Mark 8:33).

This exchange of words further illuminates the nature of temptation for us. From James' letter we learned that temptation works through our selfish carnal desires. From this dialogue between Jesus and Peter and Jesus and the devil, we see that temptation is present when we look out for man's interests or our own interest even when those interests conflict with God's plans and strategies.

Consequently, we can see that to serve self's interests when those interests do not coincide with God's is to succumb to the devil's temptations.

Let us repeat here that God's desire for each one of us is that we come into maximum fulfillment and enter into a life of great blessedness and success. It is only those who put His interests above their own carnal desires and self-seeking ways who can inherit this long-term blessedness in His time and way.

Times of temptation are permitted in our lives so that we may face up to what is within us and deliberately choose to put God's interests and ways above our own. Even if that should mean short-term loss and humiliation, we know that in the end it will be the happiest way for us also. If anyone chooses to take such a path of integrity and faithfulness, God will guarantee that in due time all of those good things that he was willing to forfeit for the sake of obedience to Him, will be added in the right time and way.

Obedience to God's leadings will at times involve tough choices for all who want to be disciples of Jesus. These choices may involve us in short-term losses, but in due season they will result in enduring rewards.

"If any man would come after me, let him deny himself and take up his cross and follow me. For whoever would save his life will lose it; and whoever loses his life for my sake and the gospel's will save it. For what does it profit a man to gain the whole world and forfeit his life?"

says Jesus (Mark 8:34-37).

Later He says: *"Truly, I say to you, there is no one who has left house or brothers or sisters or mother or father or children or lands for my sake and for the gospel, who will not receive a hundredfold now in this time, houses and brothers and sisters and mothers and children and lands, with persecutions, and in the age to come eternal life. But many that are first will be last and the last first"* (Mark 10:29-31).

In these passages, Jesus is showing us that God has no objection to our possessing power and land in this life, but that when there is conflict between the demands of these things and the demands of God and His gospel, obedience to God must come first. Furthermore, He assures us that whenever this radical obedience to the call of God and the standards of His kingdom causes loss, then in time God will more than compensate for the loss. In fact He will repay a hundredfold.

"Beloved, I wish above all things that thou mayest prosper and be in health, even as thy soul prospereth" (III John 1:2). Prosperity is God's will for His people. By this we mean that He provides His children with all they need to live efficiently on this earth and without financial bondage and anxiety.

John links our prosperity to the prosperity of our souls. If we have great material prosperity, it will be worthless and empty if it is not accompanied by a prosperity in our souls. Our external success is to be the outflow of the prosperity of our souls, and our souls cannot prosper if we pursue self-gratification rather than obedience to God.

Our souls can only prosper as we die to self through obedience to the Spirit. God wants us to prosper, but not at the expense of our souls. Those who pursue God's will as their highest goal will find themselves abundantly supplied in every area by their heavenly Father.

There is a journey to be made between the promises of God and their fulfillment that can only be made through the pathway of obedience. The devil tempts us to pursue the promises without taking the pathway of obedience and to miss God in the process. The choices that Jesus made in the wilderness must be made by each one of us if we are to come after him. Jesus allowed the devil to expose every tendency to evil that was in Himself. Then He faced up to those weaknesses and decided not to be ruled by them.

This decision which He took at the beginning of His public ministry caused Him to be sensitive to any recurrence of these temptations amidst the business of the hectic years of His public ministry. Because He had faced these temptations head-on in the lonely silence of the desert, He was able to recognize them later as they would reoccur and not be seduced by them.

Obedience was to be His pathway to His glorious position and success and not the pursuit of success itself or the trappings of success. *"Let each of you look not only to his own interests, but also to the interests of others. Have this mind among yourselves which you have in Christ Jesus, who, though he was in the form of God, did not count equality with God a thing to be grasped, but emptied himself, taking the form of a servant, being born in the likeness of men. And being found in human form, he humbled himself and became obedient unto death, even death on a cross.*

"Therefore God has highly exalted him and bestowed on him the name which is above every name, that at the name of Jesus every knee should bow, in heaven and on earth and under the earth, and every tongue con-

fess that Jesus Christ is Lord, to the glory of God the Father" (Philippians 2:4-11).

For a brief moment, it seemed that the path of obedience was a path of total loss, but in the long run, it resulted in ultimate, permanent victory and exaltation for Jesus.

The choices which Jesus made in His days in moments of temptation are to be made by all of us, especially those who have been anointed with His Spirit. The battle over the devil and self has already been won by Jesus for all of us, but it is to be lived out and worked out in our lives through simple obedience. All expediency and short-term gain must be put in second place to the leading of the Holy Spirit in the lives of all disciples. In the end, possibly after great short-term loss, God will bring vindication and enduring honor to all who have been willing to heed His voice above every other clamor.

A Prayer

Yes, Lord; I decide to follow you that your plans for my life may be fulfilled. Cause me to be faithful to you, and to follow you faithfully. I know that as I seek obedience and faithfulness to you, everything else in my life will fall into place. Amen.

CHAPTER 13

OVERCOMING TEMPTATION

In the previous chapter we saw how temptation works through our lustful desires and how the object of temptation is usually something that God may want to give anyway in His own time. Now we want to look at the source of our vulnerability to temptation. When we recognize where the source of this weakness is, we can more easily overcome temptation.

The temptations with which the devil tempted Jesus were prefaced with a little phrase designed to place doubt in Jesus' mind: *"If you are the Son of God..."* (Matthew 4:3). The devil tried to inject doubt and then demanded that Jesus should do something to dispel the doubt and prove who He was.

Jesus answered by quoting the written Word of God. Jesus was the Son of God and always will be. He did not have to prove it. He did not need the acclaim of people, material prosperity, or mighty miracles to prove that He was who He was. He knew that He was the Son of God and that God had appointed Him to be heir of all things.

"In many and various ways God spoke of old to our fathers by the prophets; but in these last days he has spoken to us by a Son, whom he appointed the heir of all things, through whom also he created the world" (Hebrews 1:1-3).

Jesus knew who He was and what His inheritance was. The temptation was to attempt to cause Him first to doubt who He was and then to try to make Him pursue what was already His and, thus, to get Him to live in a separated position from His Father.

Once we are born from above, we too have become partakers of the divine nature. There may be no evidence for our belief that we are now sons of God through the new birth and joint heirs with Jesus except the written Word of God and our belief in it.

When Jesus was in the wilderness, He had no evidence to indicate that He was the Son of God and the one that God had appointed to be heir of all things other than His belief in who He was according to the written Word of God. He did not look like the Messiah. He did not look like one who was living in God's abundant material provision nor did He look like the appointed King of the whole earth. But He was, and is, all of these things even though the external visible evidence was not yet manifest.

After he had overcome the temptation to doubt who He was and respond to doubt by attempting to prove or become that which He already was, He returned to Galilee to conduct His public ministry in the power of the Spirit and in obedience to His Father. He entered His public ministry not to attain a name or to become the heir of all things, but He embarked on this ministry knowing that He was already all of this with the pure motive to serve.

"You know that the rulers of the Gentiles lord it over them, and their great men exercise authority over them. It shall not be so among you; but whoever would be great among you must be your servant, and whoever would be first among you must be your slave; even as the Son of man came not to be served but to serve, and to give His life as a ransom for many" (Matthew 20:25-28).

When you and I become really established in the knowledge of who we really are in virtue of our position in Christ, we shall be released from looking for the evidence of who we are from our circumstances or from the opinions of others. The written scriptures, the witness of the Holy Spirit and our faith in the work of Jesus are all the evidence we need.

Without faith it is impossible to please God (Hebrews 11:6). Only by drawing from God's own resources and by allowing Him to establish His own work and Word, can we please Him. That which is not of faith is sin (Romans 14:23).

All Jesus' actions were to proceed from the Father. He was to do nothing of His own initiative but only to do and to say that which the Father would do and say through Him. The Father would establish His own plans through Jesus and establish Jesus in His plans. *"Truly, truly, I say to you, the Son can do nothing of His own accord, but only what He sees the Father doing; for whatever He does, that the Son does likewise....I can do nothing on my own authority; as I hear, I judge; and my judgement is just because I seek not my own will but the will of him who sent me"* (John 5:19 & 30).

The temptations that all believers have to overcome is the temptation to doubt who they now are in Christ and what their inheritance in Him is. When we doubt these things we can be easily drawn off course to try to prove who we are, or to strive after that which is already held by God in trust for us. God's Word is established forever and those who remain in the rest of faith will experience God establishing His Word in their lives. *"I am watching over my word to perform it"* (Jeremiah 1:12).

Peter sums up how we are to resist and overcome temptation in times of trial and suffering. In such times only our faith and not our circumstances is confirming God's Word. *"Humble yourselves therefore under the mighty hand of God, that in due time he may exalt you. Cast all your anxieties on him, for he cares about you. Be sober, be watchful. Your adversary the devil prowls around like a roaring lion seeking someone to devour. Resist him, firm in your faith, knowing that the same experience of suffering is required of your brotherhood throughout the world. And after you have suffered a little while, the God of all grace who has called you to his eternal glory in Christ will himself restore, establish and strengthen you"* (I Peter 5:6-10).

Let us not doubt who we now are through Christ or the reality of our Father's glorious plan for us even when we have to wait for its unfolding. As we abide in Him and refuse to be drawn off course through doubt or impatience into self-exaltation, He Himself will exalt us and fulfill His own great plans for us.

CHAPTER 14

THE FULNESS OF REDEMPTION
FOR SOUL AND BODY

The salvation of our spirits comes about in an instant as soon as we put our faith in God's work through Jesus on the cross and receive the forgiveness of our sins and a new heart. When we receive the Spirit of Christ into our hearts we have a new Spirit and our spirits are saved.

After we have been saved in spirit, we must now allow the Holy Spirit to change our minds and attitudes (souls) so that we truly take on the mind of Christ. This is the work of sanctification. It is not enough for us to be saved in spirit; we must also allow our attitudes, thoughts and actions to be changed by the Holy Spirit and our cooperation with Him.

Unfortunately, many Christian do not progress from the foundation of the salvation of their spirits and the forgiveness of their sins to put on the mind and attitude of Christ.

Most of the New Testament is written to people who

are already saved in spirit. These writings are filled with exhortations, advice and revelations which are aimed at bringing those who are already saved in spirit into an on-goingsalvation of their souls. Let us now take a closer look at this most important part of our redemption, the salvation of our souls or minds.

"Therefore put away all filthiness and rank growth of wickedness and receive with meekness the implanted word which is able to save your souls" (James 1:21).

"I appeal to you therefore, brethren, by the mercies of God, to present your bodies as a living sacrifice, holy and acceptable to God which is your spiritual worship. Do not be conformed to this world but be transformed by the renewal of your mind (soul) *that you may prove what is the will of God, what is good and acceptable and per-fect"* (Romans 12:1-2).

"If any man would come after me, let him deny him-self and take up his cross and follow me. For whoever would save his life will lose it; and whoever loses his life for my sake and the gospel's wall save it. For what does it profit a man to gain the whole world and forfeit his life (soul)?" (Mark 8:34-36).

The work of the transformation of our souls is a co-operative adventure with us and the Holy Spirit. It is a venture that moves on several different fronts as the en-grafted Word of God changes our attitudes and perspectives.

The believer who wishes to be like Jesus must be willing to take every thought captive to Christ. With the help of the Holy Spirit, he must put away from himself every thought and attitude that is contrary to the nature and teaching of Christ. This is a mind renewal process which takes place as the Holy Spirit teaches us the words of Jesus and opens our eyes to understand His message.

Our value system changes when we come into relationship with God through Christ. We begin to take on His mercy and gentleness; we begin to understand that He controls our destiny and we begin to learn to cease from restless striving. We begin to have a deeper faith and trust and to see life from an entirely different perspective.

As we allow the Holy Spirit to teach us and to make the teaching of Jesus alive to us, we change the way we conduct our lives. Our attitude towards frustration and success change. As we yield to these changes and submit to the new way of living that the Holy Spirit is trying to lead us into, our minds are being changed.

It is a wonderful experience to have our attitudes to so many things change, and to come into agreement with the truth as revealed by the Spirit and the Word. Jesus promised that when the Holy Spirit came, He would *"teach you all things, and bring to your remembrance all that I have said to you"* (John 14:26).

As the Holy Spirit engrafts the Words of Jesus into us and makes them real to us, and as we obey these words, our attitudes are changed to conform to Christ's mind. Our minds are being changed to conform to the truth and to come into oneness with God. Our spirits have become united with God at the new birth and our minds are being renewed as we receive, surrender, and obey the Word of God.

Our minds have been programmed according to certain patterns of thought and action by the world and environment in which we live. As the Word of God becomes alive to us through the work of the Holy Spirit, our value system changes. Our old value system may have been good and noble, but when the Holy Spirit comes, He still has many many changes to make in the way we think, act, and respond.

"For as the heavens are higher than the earth, so are my ways higher than your ways and my thoughts than your thoughts" (Isaiah 55:9). The ways of God are much higher than the conventional wisdom of our society. As we allow our attitudes and behavior to be transformed to conform no longer to the way of our society, but to conform instead to the ways of the kingdom that Jesus reveals, we are transformed in a progressive way.

Grumbling is replaced with praise; sorrow with laughter; bitterness with forgiveness and love; and despair replaced with joyful anticipation. How important it is for us to really allow the Holy Spirit and the Word of God to wash and renew our minds. How important it is for us to put on the new perspectives and attitudes of the kingdom.

New Creation (Positive) Thinking

The renewing of the mind or soul also involves renewing our self-image. Our actions are controlled to a very large extent by our self-image. *"For as he thinketh in his heart, so is he"* (Proverbs 23:7 KJV). Our thinking controls the way we act and live. Thus, it is vital for us to have a renewed thought life. Of course, thinking in itself is not sufficient unless those thoughts are true. The renewed thinking of the Christian is *much more than mere positive* thinking.

There once was a man who believed strongly in positive thinking. He believed that he could be everything he thought he could be and do everything he thought he could do. Once he went on a skydiving expedition. He believed he could jump safely from the airplane if he thought strongly enough about it. He persuaded himself through much positive affirmations that he could fly from the airplane, and finally, he jumped. The results were disastrous.

His companion, a more cautious man, attached a parachute to his shoulders before attempting to jump. He had great difficulty in summoning enough courage to jump. He did not want to be fearful but he somehow could not overcome it. There was fear in his mind that he could not easily expel. Finally, he tried to think positively. He had heard much about it from his friend.

"I know I can jump. I know I can jump safely. I know I can jump safely," he thought within himself crowding out the welling thoughts of fear that had been programmed into him over a lifetime. "I know I can jump safely because the parachute is securely attached."

At last he jumped and landed safely on the ground. His positive thinking was grounded on the fact that it was now safe for him to jump because he was safely secured to the parachute.

What before would have been most unsafe had now become safe because the parachute had been attached. His natural instincts like any normal human being's were conditioned by an unbuilt caution with respect to heights. However, the parachute gave him a new relationship with the law of gravity. With the parachute connected, he could begin to think differently about his relationship with gravity and the danger of jumping. Indeed, it would be necessary for him to do so if the parachute were to be used and of any use to him.

Christian positive thinking is always *grounded on the real facts*. Faith is never wishful thinking. It is always based on realities. *"Now faith is the assurance of things hoped for, the conviction of things not seen"* (Hebrews 11:1). Our faith is built on real solid facts...the facts of what God has done, the promises of God and of the Word of God.

The positive thinking of the Christian is based on solid facts and is never presumptive. Our positive thoughts are based on facts that are unseen, facts of the unseen order which the Spirit and the Word make known to us. Our senses and feelings may give us certain information about a situation or about who we are. The Word of God as revealed by the Spirit gives us much fuller information and tells us what we would not otherwise know.

The Christian's renewed mind lets its thoughts be formed, not by wishes, but by the facts of who he now is. If we still think of ourselves in the same way as we thought of ourselves before we received the very life of God to be our life, we will act according to our old identity and not according to our new identity.

"If any one is in Christ, he is a new creation; the old has passed away; behold the new has come" (2 Corinthians 5:17). A Christian has become a different kind of person when the life of Christ comes into his heart. He has a new heart and a new spirit, he has a new relationship with God and with the world. *The renewing of the mind is the process by which the mind reprograms itself by the Spirit revealed Word of God to this new identity.* This is most important, because if through lack of teaching or lack of surrender or for some other reason, a person should fail to do this, he will live far short of the life that God has won him for.

The following may serve as an example of this and illustrates the importance of renewing our minds after we have been saved (in spirit) and adopted into the family of God.

In the United States of America in the nineteenth

century, we all know that slavery was widely practiced. The majority of the black population in the southern states were brought up as slaves and to think of themselves as slaves, not as full citizens and free men. Indeed, no matter how much they may have thought of themselves as free men, they were not.

This condition of slavery, of course, affected everything about their lives, their thoughts, their hopes, their goals and their dreams. In 1863 they received their legal emancipation. From that moment on, they were no longer slaves and it was completely illegal for anyone to keep them enslaved or try to make slaves of them. They were free men.

It took only a moment to get their emancipation, but to learn to think and act as free men took a much longer time period. For the white population to treat black people as full co-equal citizens also took a long process of re-education and attitude change.

Many of the emancipated black people still thought of themselves as slaves and second-class citizens. Thus, they did not enter into the full advantages of their new position as legal first-class citizens. Slavery had formed their self-concept and though they were now no longer slaves, it would take a long, long time for their self-image to change and for the white people's image of them to change. As long as they were considered second-class citizens and continued to consider themselves in those terms, the effects of their legal emancipation was to be very limited. It took a long and gradual process of mind renewal on behalf of both black and white for the benefits of their emancipation to be fully realized.

In a similar way, after we have become members of the royal family of God, for us to fully enter into the responsibilities and privileges of this glorious estate, our minds must be renewed to catch up with the facts of this wonderful new identity. When we become born again, we are in the world in the same relationship with God that Jesus lived in as a man.

These two aspects of the redemption of our souls (discipleship and mind renewal) are essential if we are to live in the kingdom of God in the manner that Jesus has made possible for us.

The final phase of the outworking of our redemption consists in the redemption of our bodies and maturing as sons of God. . This will not be entered into by the church until the time of Jesus' return. Every Christian should be longing for this and hoping eagerly for it, that by the working of God's grace and power and by faithful cooperation he may be brought to this maturity.

"I consider that the sufferings of this present time are not worthy to be compared with the glory that is to be revealed to us. The anxious longing of creation waits eagerly for the revealing of the sons of God. Creation was subjected to futility, not of its own will but because of Him who has subjected it in the hope that the creation itself will be set free from its slavery to corruption into the freedom of the glory of the children of God.

"We know that the whole creation has been groaning in travail together until now; and not only the creation, but we ourselves, who have the first fruits of the Spirit, groan inwardly as we wait for adoption as sons, the redemption of our bodies. For in this hope, we were saved. Now hope that is seen is not hope. For who hopes for what he sees? But if we hope for what we do not see, we will wait for it with patience" (Romans 8:18-25).

Death is furthermore described in the scriptures as *"the last enemy to be overcome"* (I Corinthians 15:26). Death, then, for the Christian is something that Jesus has

conquered and overcome legally, and it is the hope of
Christians that the Holy Spirit will lead us into experiencing subjectively this final state of our redemption
when physical death will be overcome.

One of Jesus' last words to His disciples before He
returned to the Father was that it was not for us to know
the times and seasons which the Father has fixed by His
own authority (Acts 1:7). This was in reference to His return. It is the generation that will be alive and remaining
at the return of the Lord that will be the high privilege of
entering into this experience of being led by the Holy
Spirit into overcoming the last enemy, death.

Paul, in the fifteenth chapter of Corinthians, as-
sociates the overcoming of the last enemy with the blow-
ing of the last trump, at the time of Christ's return.

It is often assumed that the resurrection of the
saints, frequently referred to as *the rapture,* is an automatic experience for believers. Those who are to overcome the last enemy by the grace of God will be those
who have been living overcoming lives, overcoming the
world, the flesh and the devil.

We believe that all the signs of the times (especially
the sign of the end of gentile damnation of the nation of
Israel as foretold by Jesus in Luke 21:24) point to this
generation as the one that will welcome back the Lord
Jesus to His rightful position as manifest Lord of this
earth. It is most important that Christians today learn to
live the overcoming life so that we can be ready and waiting for the fulfillment of our redemption.

So we see that God moves progressively in our redemption. First comes Justification, which we enter into
in a moment. Then comes Sanctification which we enter
into progressively followed by Glorification, the goal of
our redemption into which the overcoming Christians

who are alive at the time of Jesus' return will enter.

"May the God of peace himself sanctify you wholly; and may your spirit and soul and body be kept sound and blameless at the coming of our Lord Jesus Christ" (I Thessalonians 5:23).

CHAPTER 15

STAGES TO PERFECTION PREFIGURED IN THE JEWISH FEASTS

The Christian life is progressive. It begins with our acceptance of the forgiveness of our sins through the work of Jesus on the cross and of the new birth. We must accept that when we receive Him, we accept the gift of New Life. It progresses from this new birth all the way to a glorious perfection.

Like all births, the new birth is but a beginning. Tragically in the church, we have for the most part been content to introduce people to the new birth as an end in itself rather than as a beginning of a spiritual adventure. The result of this neglect is that in many cases our churches have become spiritual kindergartens rather than dynamic centers of spiritual growth.

There is a definite goal to the growth process that begins with the new birth. That goal is maturity or perfection. Just as there is a goal or end to the biological growth process that begins with conception, so too our spiritual growth is bringing us towards a definite maturity. At that point, we who are now children of God will have become mature sons of God.

<u>The Stages of Christian Growth
and the Jewish Feasts</u>

As biological growth progresses through various definite stages, the same is true with spiritual growth and development. The seven major stages of Christian development are:

(1) The covering of sin through the blood of Jesus.
(2) The laying aside of our old nature through the cross of Jesus.
(3) The receiving of the new life of the Spirit within our spirits.

NOTE: Each of these stages occur virtually simultaneously in the lives of most believers.

(4) The receiving of the Baptism with the Holy Spirit which is our personal experience of Pentecost through which we receive the anointing of the Spirit to empower us to follow in the footsteps of Jesus.
(5) A progressive moving on in God through obedience and living out the overcoming life.
(6) The putting off of the last vestiges of sin through deeper surrender and the refining fire of the Holy Spirit.
(7) Receiving the manifest victory over death itself and our glorious redeemed, immortal bodies.

These stages of spiritual growth are anticipated in the ancient Jewish feasts. The seven major Jewish feasts given by God to Moses correspond exactly to the seven stages of spiritual growth we have listed above.

They are: (1) Passover. (2) Unleavened Bread. (3) First Fruits, (each of these occur in the springtime of the year and are clustered together in one holy season). (4) Feast of Weeks, also known as Pentecost because it comes fifty days after Passover usually occurring in the early summer at the time of the early barley crop. (5) Feast of Trumpets (Rosh Hoshanna). (6) Day of Atonement. (7) Feast of Tabernacles, also known as the Feast of Booths. These last three days are grouped together into one holy season at the end of the harvest year.

The Passover Stage of the Christian

The first three feasts, Passover, Unleavened Bread and First Fruits, commemorate the events of the Exodus when the Jewish people were rescued by the blood of the passover lamb, escaped Egypt and began their journey toward the promised land of Canaan.

The annual Passover feast pointed back to this great event and forward to an even greater event which it foreshadowed: Jesus' death and resurrection. His death and resurrection is the fulfillment of the Old Testament Passover. These feasts are anticipations of greater realities. As stated in the letter to the Hebrews: *"the law has but a shadow of the good things to come instead of the true form of these realities",* (Hebrews 10:1) and so the feasts of the Old Law anticipate even greater events and realities than those they commemorate.

The Passover which commemorates the Exodus has its objective fulfillment in Jesus' death and resurrection and its subjective fulfillment in the life of each believer who puts his faith in what Jesus had done. When anyone accepts Jesus as their eternal Passover Lamb, he receives the Blood of Jesus as the covering of his sins. When a believer puts his faith on Jesus' death as the death of the sin nature, he fulfills the Feast of Unleavened Bread because in Jesus' death he can put to death the leaven of his old sin nature. Whenever a believer puts his faith in the resurrection of Jesus, he can receive new life from Him and so the Feast of First Fruits is fulfilled in his life since he now has the first fruits of his redemption.

The Pentecost Stage of the Christian

The Feast of Pentecost was a time when the ancient Jewish people celebrated the early summer crop. It also commemorated the giving of the law at Mount Sinai. From that day, the people of Israel were led by the law. The New Testament Feast of Pentecost celebrates the giving of the Holy Spirit to be the law within our hearts and to be the guide of the church. The law is now replaced by the Holy Spirit who has come to be directly involved in every part of the believers' life and conduct.

Pentecost had its *objective* fulfillment on the day when God poured out His Spirit on the believers on the Feast of Pentecost following Jesus' ascension. Pentecost has its *subjective* fulfillment in the life of any believer whenever a born again believer accepts the anointing of the Holy Spirit from Jesus the Baptizer.

When the Holy Spirit is given control of our lives, He leads us in the footsteps of Jesus and into all truth. There is more and more for us to enter into even after we have been baptized by Jesus with the Holy Spirit. The Baptism with the Holy Spirit is not an end, but only the beginning of a life of obedience and ongoing change and discovery in the kingdom of God.

"I have yet many things to say to you, but you cannot bear them now." says Jesus. *"When the Spirit of truth*

comes, he will guide you into all the truth; for he will not speak on his own authority, but whatever he hears he will speak, and he will declare to you the things that are to come. He will glorify me, for he will take what is mine and declare it to you." (John 16:12-14) Jesus was promising here that the coming of the Holy Spirit would be the beginning of many discoveries for His disciples.

The Feast of Trumpets In The Life Of The Christian

The Old Testament Feast of Trumpets is a feast when trumpets are sounded summoning people to get ready for the days that are ahead. The feast of trumpets in the life of the Christian is fulfilled when we spiritually hear the call to move on in the Spirit, to prepare for spiritual battles and conquests and to get ready for the fulness of our personal redemption and the return of Christ to receive and establish His kingdom on earth.

The trumpets of the Old Testament were trumpets which summoned people to prepare for things to come and to prepare for war. We fulfill the feast of trumpets when we allow the Holy Spirit to rouse us to be alert and ready for the return of the Lord and to be actively hastening the day of His coming. We fulfill this feast also when we do not rest on the laurels of the new birth and the Baptism with the Holy Spirit, but press on through greater and greater surrender, to perfection.

Trumpets is the place of getting ready, counting the cost, waking up from our religious complacency and getting ready for an even greater hour in the church and an even greater fulfillment of our redemption.

"Therefore gird up your minds, be sober, set your hope fully upon the grace that is coming to you at the revelation of Jesus Christ." (I Peter 1:13) Peter here is

sounding the trumpet note to his readers. Paul, too, shows that he has heard that trumpet calling him up- ward and onward when he writes: *"Not that I have al- ready obtained this or am already perfect; but I press on to make it my own, because Christ Jesus has made me his own. Brethren, I do not consider that I have made it my own; but one thing I do, forgetting what lies behind and straining forward to what lies ahead, I press on toward the goal for the prize of the upward call of God in Christ Jesus."* (Philippians 3:12-15)

"Therefore let us leave the elementary doctrines of Christ and go on to maturity, not laying again a founda- tion of repentance from dead works and of faith toward God, with instruction about ablutions, the laying on of hands, the resurrection of the dead, and eternal judg- ment." (Hebrews 6:1-2)

Here again the trumpet note is being sounded to the church to move on from the elementary things toward the perfection to which we are called. We are not to leave these foundations behind in the sense that we do not need them any more or that they are beneath us, but we are to build on the foundation of what we have already entered into through Christ.

The Atonement Stage In The Christians Progress

The Feast of Trumpets is followed by the Atonement Day. On this day, the High Priest would take two goats, one of which was to be slain as an atonement sacrifice and the other to be driven out into the wilderness.

At first sight we may wonder why the Day of Atone- ment is placed at this part of the year. One would expect that the issue of atonement would have been settled at the Passover Feast. It is true that the blood of Jesus shed on Calvary, which is the New Testament fulfillment of Passover, settles the issue of the forgiveness of our sins. The Lord, however, wants to go even further than forgiving our sins, He wants to put all sin out of our lives completely. The driving of one of the goats out into the wilderness on the Day of Atonement anticipates the final work of the Lord of removing all sin from His people. The scriptures tell us that Jesus is coming for a bride without spot or wrinkle, and so His coming is preceded by an intense purifying of the church.

It was to believers who were at this stage of their Christian development that Peter was referring to when he wrote: *"Beloved do not be surprised at the fiery ordeal which comes upon you to prove you, as though something strange were happening to you. But rejoice in so far as you share Christ's sufferings, that you may also rejoice and be glad when his glory is revealed. If you are reproached for the name of Christ, you are blessed, because the spirit of glory and of God rests upon you. But let none of you suffer as a murderer, or a thief, or a wrongdoer, or a mischief-maker; yet if one suffers as a Christian, let him not be ashamed, but under that name let him glorify God. For the time has come for judgement to begin with the household of God; and if it begins with us, what will be that end of those who do not obey the gospel of God?"* (I Peter 4:12-17)

Peter has been urging his readers to get ready for the Lord's return. The suffering that they are going through is not a judgement of condemnation, but a crisis for their purification. This is the atonement (refining) stage in our progress as Christians, and it prepares us for the final harvest of our personal redemption and for the triumphant return of Jesus.

There are certain forms of suffering which the Christian is exempt from, and which he does well to resist. There is however another form of suffering, which is a suffering of purification. This can come in any form the Lord allows, and to resist in this case would be to resist God. This is an important area for discernment. We need to know how to resist the devil and all that he would throw against us, but we also need to know to do what Peter urges us to do when he writes: *"Humble yourselves therefore under the mighty hand of God, that in due time He may exalt you."* (I Peter 5:6) This process in our spiritual advance corresponds to the Jewish feast of Atonement, that is, it fulfills in reality what the feast foreshadows.

It is important that we see this Atonement purification stage as only a transition stage in the process of being led to full maturity by the Holy Spirit. This stage is preparing us for a greater revelation of the glory of God. *"This slight momentary affliction is preparing us for an eternal weight of glory beyond all comparison."* (II Corinthians 4:17) *"...looking to Jesus the pioneer and perfector of our faith, who for the joy that was set before him endured the cross, despising the shame."* (Hebrews 12:2)

The suffering of refinement is a preparation for a great revelation of God's glory to us and in us. As God prepares us for the final stages of our redemption, the heat of the refiner's fire is felt with greater intensity. This is not the suffering of sin, defeat or unbelief, but the suffering of those who are being refined by the fire of the Holy Spirit. Jesus baptizes us with the Holy Spirit and with fire. This refining fire cleanses us of all impurities and fleshiness to get us ready for the return of the Lord, and for the final phase of our redemption. John the Baptist had said: *"I baptize you with water for repentance, but he who is coming after me is mightier than I, whose sandals I am not worthy to carry; he will baptize you with the Holy Spirit AND WITH FIRE. His winnowing fork is in his hand, and he will clear his threshing floor and gather his wheat into the granary, but the chaff he will burn with unquenchable fire."* (Matthew 3:11-12) This fire burns the chaff of impurity out of the lives of those who are moving on in Christ and getting ready for the *glory that is to be revealed.*

The Feast Of Tabernacles
The Final Stage Of Our Redemption

The Feast of Tabernacles is the final and most joyful of the Jewish feasts. It is the only Old Testament feast that has not been fulfilled in the New Testament - YET. A fulfillment of this feast is anticipated by the New Testament writers, however. Christians, though they have experienced the fulfillment of Passover and Pentecost, are still awaiting an even more glorious moment in history. At that time, He who came first as a lamb will return in triumph; and we who now have the first fruits of the Spirit will come forth into the fulness of our redemption.

This final stage of our redemption will bring us to full maturity in Christ. Now the nature of Christ in every born again believer is partly hidden by the veil of our own flesh. When the fulness of our redemption comes to us, the veil of our flesh will no longer hide the glory of Christ in us.

Paul speaks of *"Christ in you, the hope of glory".* (Colossians 1:27) This indicates that the presence of Christ in us is a promise of an even greater glory. The gift of the Holy Spirit is not the end but the downpayment on an even greater glory that is to be revealed in us at the right time. We have already received the Holy Spirit, but *the best is yet to be* for us who believe.

As wonderful as the new birth is, as joyous as the Pentecost gift of the Holy Spirit is, there is yet a greater stage of our redemption ahead of us. It is in this hope that we have been saved.

The gifts of forgiveness, new birth and the baptism in the Holy Spirit can be received through faith; but the full breaking out of this glory in us and the full redemption of our bodies is not something that can be claimed by faith, but something for which we should all HOPE.

Paul writes: *"I consider that the sufferings of this present time are not worth comparing with the glory that is to be revealed to us. For the creation waits with eager longing for the revealing of the sons of God;....We know that the whole creation has been groaning in travail together until now; and not only the creation but we ourselves, who have the first fruits of the Spirit, groan inwardly as we wait for adoption as sons, the redemption of our bodies. For in this hope we were saved."* (Romans 8:18-19,22-24)

This is the great event that is pre-figured by the Jewish Feast of Tabernacles. During this feast the Jews celebrate the full harvest. It is the festival of greatest joy in which they celebrate the conclusion of the agricultural year. It points to a time when Jesus comes to harvest those who have obeyed Him to the very end.

Throughout the feast the Jewish people live in little booths which they construct and cover with branches of various trees and decorate with fruit. The feast of booths anticipates a time when the glory of God will swallow up even the death that is in our bodies and a time when all of us will have fellowship with God in a richer way than ever.

The goal, or full harvest of our redemption will be a

time when we who have the first fruits of the Holy Spirit will attain to the complete harvest of our redemption, the redemption of our bodies and our manifestation as mature sons of God. This is the goal of our redemption and the hope of our glory for which we hope with a sure and eager hope.

The feast of Passover was fulfilled by Jesus in the "fulness of time". Jesus came at a time that was preordained by the Father, not a day sooner or later. His death on the cross in the thirty-third year of His life on earth came on a Passover that was preordained. Jesus knew that His hour had come.

The promise of the Jewish feast of Pentecost was also fulfilled at precisely the right time, *when the day of Pentecost was fully come.* God inhabits eternity but moves with precise timing in the history of man. Before the death and resurrection of Jesus, no one could receive the new birth because, as John says, *"as yet the Spirit had not been given."* (John 7:39) Before the day of Pentecost that followed Jesus' resurrection, no one could receive the *Baptism with the Holy Spirit.* The final stage of our redemption will likewise be revealed at a precise moment in history.

All Christians joyfully await the objective return and appearing of Jesus. This will be the objective fulfillment in history of the Feast of Tabernacles.

Paul wrote that the great goal of his life was: to *"know him and the power of his resurrection, and may share in his sufferings, becoming like him in death, that if possible I may attain the resurrection from the dead. Not that I have already obtained this or am already perfect (complete); but I press on to make it my own, because Christ Jesus has made me his own. Brethren, I do not consider that I have made it my own; but one thing I do, forgetting what lies behind and straining forward to what lies ahead, I press on toward the goal for the prize of the upward call of God is Christ Jesus."* (Philippians 3:10-14).

Peter says that we are guarded by God's power *"through faith for a salvation ready to be revealed in the last time"* (I Peter 1:5). Since his readers had already experienced both the Passover and Pentecost dimension of their salvation, he is referring here to the final stage of our salvation which will break forth in the last days when immortality and glory will be experienced by the most humble and eager members of the church.

All who have entered the Passover and Pentecost dimension of salvation should be eagerly preparing themselves for this glorious event when the sons of God will be fully manifested and anointed and attain to the fulness of redemption. From the signs of the times (especially the times of the gentiles being fulfilled by the return of Jerusalem to the Jews, Luke 21:24), we have every reason to believe that this generation will be the one that will experience Jesus' fulfilling the Jewish Feast of Tabernacles and personally experience resurrection.

Just as the generation that was alive to witness the resurrection of Jesus was the first generation to be able to enter into the kingdom of God through the new birth and be able to receive the Baptism with the Holy Spirit, so the generation that witnesses the return of Jesus will be the one that receives the fulness of redemption.

Just as the whole generation that was alive at the time of Jesus' resurrection did not receive the Holy Spirit because of disbelief, so we do not expect all to enter into the completion of their redemption at the time of Jesus' return though this dimension will be opened up for all who are eager and watchful and obedient.

Summary and Conclusion

The feasts of the ancient Israelites which are still celebrated by devout Jews today, provide us with a perfect type and prefiguring of the stages of redemption in the life of a New Testament believer. Too often in the church we have made a plateau of one of these stages, the stage of the new birth, for example, or the stage of the Baptism with the Holy Spirit. The time has come, however, for the church to build on these foundations and to press toward the perfection and complete redemption that the Spirit is preparing us for which is to be attained at the time of Jesus' return.

The Christian faith is not only a faith, but it is also a blessed hope. Faith builds on the foundation of the finished work of Jesus; hope catches a vision of the greater glory that is yet to be revealed. We believe the Body of Chirst on the earth today is being summoned to prepare to be led into realms of victory and glory that surpass anything attained to by previous generations of Christians.

At the right time this final stage of redemption that is anticipated by the Jewish Feast of Tabernacles, will be revealed. *"When he appears we shall be like him for we shall see him as he is."* (I John 3:2)

The new birth is only a beginning; Pentecost, or the Baptism with the Holy Spirit is not the end. God is summoning us to a greater closeness to Himself, to holiness, and to prepare for the glory that is soon to be revealed. Let us be among those who *"by patience in well-doing seek for glory and honor and immortality."* (Romans 2:7)

This is the challenge to the overcomers. Have you accepted it?